Mainstreaming Emotionally Disturbed Children

SYRACUSE SPECIAL EDUCATION AND REHABILITATION
MONOGRAPH SERIES, 10

Mainstreaming
Emotionally Disturbed
Children

A. J. PAPPANIKOU and JAMES L. PAUL, *Editors*

 SYRACUSE UNIVERSITY PRESS   1977

Library of Congress Cataloging in Publication Data
Main entry under title:

Mainstreaming emotionally disturbed children.

    (Syracuse special education and rehabilitation monograph series; 10)
    Includes bibliographies and index.
    1. Mentally ill children—Education—Addresses, essays, lectures. I. Pappanikou, A. J. II. Paul, James L. III. Series: Syracuse University. Special education and rehabilitation monograph series; 10.
LC4165.M34   371.9'4   76-54730
ISBN 0-8156-0131-X

This manuscript was developed pursuant to Grant #OE-9-167016-3573(725) from the Bureau for Educational Personnel Development, United States Office of Education, Department of Health, Education and Welfare. The opinions expressed herein do not necessarily reflect the position or the policy of the United States Office of Education, and no official endorsement by the United States Office of Education should be inferred.

Manufactured in the United States of America

Foreword

W<small>ITH THE PUBLICATION</small> of this volume we begin to find some substance to the concept of mainstreaming, a point of view that has swept public education, oftentimes in violent forms, in the past few years. Mainstreaming frequently has been adopted on the basis of frustrations with the way things have been, with inadequacies in both general and special education teacher preparation, and on the basis of publications which did little more than to provide case studies of situations in which mainstreaming was purported to be successful.

Concrete, objective, and longitudinal data which would validate mainstreaming versus other forms of educational management are still lacking. In this book, however, is a set of authors who individually and collectively have studied the issues of mainstreaming, and who, out of their broad backgrounds and long experiences in the field of professional education, are able to view the problem objectively. Their study has lead them to conceptualize a number of important theoretical positions which are vital to the implementation of a program for emotionally disturbed children in community education.

Mainstreaming as an educational policy is undoubtedly one of the most difficult types of programs to implement. It requires a unanimity of thinking and understanding at all levels of public education, from members of boards of education to administrators to teachers to ancillary personnel and to support personnel. It requires changes in attitudes toward exceptional children on the part of many educators who are motivated by fears, guilt feelings, and misinformation regarding not only emotionally disturbed children, but many other clinical types of exceptional children. Mainstreaming requires a sound theoretical structure which is thoroughly understood and accepted by all those who try to carry out this philosophical approach to education.

With the passage of Public Law 94-142, "Education For All Handi-capped Children Act," the issues concerning the right of youth to have access to the "mainstream" or the "least restrictive alternative" is legally affirmed. The U.S. Congress has supported this legal commitment to exceptional children by funding this Act with an appropriation of $358 million for Fiscal Year 1978 and $3.2 billion by 1982. Unless sound theoretical foundations are laid, both effort and money could be mis-directed and wasted.

A theoretical structure is provided by the authors of this book, each a specialist on particular topics. This volume is a significant bench mark for the professional attack on the total problem. There are con-cepts in these pages which are essential to all programs of educational implementation. As noted in the chapters, the total life milieu is the child's educational structure. In a concept of mainstreaming, the total life structure for the exceptional child is one of extraordinary complex-ity. For this reason alone this volume is of significance and importance.

William M. Cruickshank, Editor
Syracuse Special Education
and Rehabilitation
Monograph Series

Contributors

William M. Cruickshank is Director of the Institute for the Study of Mental Retardation and Related Disabilities, University of Michigan, Ann Arbor, Michigan.

Albert H. Fink is Associate Professor and Coordinator of Programs for the Behaviorally Disordered, Department of Special Education and Center for Innovation and Teaching Handicapped, Indiana University, Bloomington, Indiana.

Frank M. Hewett is Professor of Education and Psychiatry at the University of California, Los Angeles.

William C. Morse is Professor of Educational Psychology and Psychology and the Chairperson of the Combined Program in Education and Psychology at the University of Michigan in Ann Arbor.

A. J. Pappanikou is Professor of Educational Psychology and Chairperson of Special Education at the University of Connecticut, Storrs, Connecticut, and Co-Director of the USOE Technical Assistance Project, "Understanding Handicapping Conditions Among Disadvantaged Children."

James L. Paul is Director of Graduate Studies in Special Education and Associate Professor of Education at the University of North Carolina at Chapel Hill, North Carolina. He is also Director of Training Developmental Disabilities Technical Assistance System, Frank Porter Graham Child Development Center, University of North Carolina.

William C. Rhodes is Professor of Psychology at the University of Michigan, Ann Arbor, Michigan.

Jerome J. Spears is Director of Pupil Personnel for the Mansfield Public School System, Mansfield, Connecticut.

H. Rutherford Turnbull III is Assistant Director of the Institute of Government and Associate Professor of Public Law and Government at the University of North Carolina at Chapel Hill. He is the Counsel to the Task Force on Limited Guardianship for the North Carolina Developmental Disabilities Council and to various state and local mental health agencies.

Richard J. Whelan is Ralph L. Smith Professor of Child Development
and Professor of Education and Pediatrics at the University of Kansas
and University of Kansas Medical Center. He is also Director of Education at the Children's Rehabilitation Unit/University Affiliated Facility at the Medical Center.

Frank H. Wood is Professor of Psycho-Educational Studies and Special Education at the University of Minnesota, Minneapolis, Minnesota.

Contents

Introduction

A. J. PAPPANIKOU

"MAINSTREAMING" IS A TERM WITH MANY DEFINITIONS, each reflecting the particular interests of those individuals and/or systems that deal with the exceptional child. While the goal of mainstreaming is to educate exceptional children in a nonsegregated physical and human environment, implementing that goal depends upon certain variables, many of which put the educational welfare of the child second to the interests of the educational establishment.

To place a child in an environment that more adequately reflects the society of which the child belongs is a goal of all education. However, to do this without considering the mutual readiness of both the child and the system is dangerous, counterproductive, and, in many cases, destructive to both the child and the system. This is true not only for exceptional youth but also for "normal" youngsters whose readiness level is out of phase with placement. For example, it is not unusual to find that chronological age, not individual readiness levels, determines expectations and, in turn, curricula for the "normal" youth, especially in reading and arithmetic. Society has come to equate "normality" with "average" academic achievement. This attitude has been put into practice by "educators" through programs that attempt to motivate each child to achieve at or above the "mean" or arithmetic average, instead of "normally" progressing according to his or her ability. Under the statistical concept of "normality," which is the basis for all standardized achievement tests, 50 percent of the youth should function above and 50 percent below the mean or "average" expected achievement for a specific group. Thus, with the exception of the severely handicapped, a clearcut demarcation between normality and abnormality is difficult to establish. Furthermore, *group* curricular and methodological considerations based upon these categories give rise to problems similar to the unrealistic readiness situation mentioned above: individualization of programs and methods is the common denominator that pervades *all* educational endeavors.

If this is the case, some argue, why do we need special education? Why should school systems stigmatize children by placing them in special education classes and thereby render them "different" when in reality they are part of the normality continuum? These questions imply not only that children placed in special education intervention programs should be mainstreamed but also that, except for the extremely handicapped, they should initially not have been placed in special programs. In other words, mainstreaming implies that the "normal" school system has developed to a state of "readiness" that will provide the individualization of instruction necessary for the academic and personal self-actualization of each and every student of that system. One implication in the concept of mainstreaming is that the "system" has already been psychologically and programmatically "mainstreamed." This is obviously not the case, for a cursory investigation of any system shows that these concepts have not yet been put into operation even for children who are considered normal but who manifest individual differences. There are those who feel that special education classes are essential in order to "protect" the exceptional child and to assure that a prescribed program, based upon intellectual and emotional ability and readiness, is offered. The only problem with this view lies in the fact that many programs tend to overemphasize the former at the expense of the latter. Johnson (1962) tended to support this conclusion. He also questioned the efficacy of special education classes for the educable retarded via a focusing on teacher qualifications and special programming. His work was the catalyst for initiating what today is known as mainstreaming. Dunn's (1968) criticism of similar classes raised more questions and provided impetus for the movement.

Hundreds of papers and thousands of presentations on the mainstreaming concept have followed these critiques of special education. Most dealt with the mentally handicapped and learning disabled child; very few were addressed to the socially and emotionally maladjusted. One might conclude that the disturbed child is "too different" and that his other needs are not related to the achievement variables used as evaluative yardsticks in the efficacy studies on mainstreaming. The major problems that these youth have are manifested by behavior which is too disturbing either to the comfort level of the teacher or to the learning sets of other children. However, disturbance or disturbing behavior could affect any child or could superimpose itself upon other disabilities, and the disturbance thus becomes primary, regardless of etiology. In view of this, many professionals viewed educational programming for these children differently in that achievement took a back seat to a curriculum that set behavioral change as its primary goal, and self-contained programs thus received more attention. But the findings of Bandura (1972) indicated that negative rather than positive behavior would be modeled with greater ease and frequency. Also the contagious effects of special education classes for these youth had not received enough consideration. Hewett's (1968) point of view that achievement is an intrinsic goal for all children, and Pappanikou and Johnson's (1974) data indicating that reading achievement is inversely correlated with disturbing behavior, supported the contention that individualized curricula and methods aimed at improving achievement could indeed be viewed as a common denominator for educating *all* children.

The positions on mainstreaming for emotionally disturbed youth became polarized. To expect education to take place in an atmosphere that was disruptive and counter-productive to both the disturbing child and his non-disturbed peers was unrealistic. To place a child with children who manifested similar disturbing behaviors would appear to reinforce and increase the probability of that behavior. Also, in such classes there is greater probability in not meeting the achievement needs of these children and thus more chance that the behavior responsible for special placement would continue. It certainly appears much easier to mainstream if a handicap is non-behavioral or is simply related to ability. Data relative to special classes tend to indicate that a majority of pupils who are placed in special classes have the concomitant disability of disturbing behavior (Bower *et al.* 1958). Any and all mainstreaming schemes should therefore contain provisions for dealing with the student's behavior as well as achievement.

There is today almost universal agreement in the field of special education that the ultimate goal is for each exceptional youth to function as independently in society as his or her ability allows. In some cases, the initial step toward this goal may be self-containment or segregation; in others, Redl and Wattenberg's (1959) on-the-spot first aid may be sufficient to maintain the student. Provisions for equal educational opportunity for all, including the handicapped, was mandated first by the courts after the educational establishment had been legally challenged.

In 1975 this became the law of the land via Public Law 94–142 ("Education of All Handicapped Children Act"). With this mandate in mind, can self-containment, even though it may be a beginning toward an optimal educational opportunity for a specific youth, be regarded as equal educational opportunity?

Is the assumption that mainstreaming is "good" for *all* youth valid? Are systems ready to initiate individual programmatic efforts on behalf of a specific handicapped child? How much assurance do the educators give that the special education individualized endeavor is not a modern Annie Inskeep (1926) "watered-down curriculum"? Are there precautions that can be taken which will not make any "restrictive alternative" (self-contained special class, resource room, etc.) a terminal placement either in reality or expectations? Is it possible to train educators, regardless of where the children are in the "normality continuum," to see that ability must replace disability as the focus for individual programs? What higher-education training model is available to change the perception of educational leadership so that the child does not have to be called "deviant" in order to benefit from the concept of special education? How do we deal with the para-educational systems, such as unions, so that they become partners rather than adversaries in the educational endeavor? Does special education have a different connotation for inner-city school systems?

These questions and concerns about mainstreaming prompted the Editors to call a meeting of experts in the education of children for whom disturbed or disturbing behavior is the primary common denominator for "normal class" exclusion. It was felt that a presentation of ideas to this limited group of colleagues would allow for dialogue among the participants and critical feedback on their concepts, models, or programs.

These participants were invited not only because of their leadership in the education of disturbed youth but also because of their ability to evolve new ideas and models in educating and preventing disabilities in *all* youth.

The conference was hosted and held at the University of Connecticut in February of 1975. Funding was provided by EPDA Grant #OE-0-167016-3573(725), "Understanding Handicapping Conditions Among Disadvantaged Children," co-directors, A. J. Pappanikou and J. F. Cawley.

Most of these participants prepared this final manuscript addressing themselves to those questions posed earlier. The intent of this book is to stimulate careful analysis of mainstreaming emotionally disturbed children. It is an attempt to encourage all who are concerned with the educational needs and rights of children to re-evaluate the present state of mainstreaming in their particular situation and, if need be, reformulate their perceptions about models, programs, and considerations presented here. This is not a how-to book on mainstreaming. It does afford to each educator ("regular" or "special"), para-educator, legal professional, and parent an opportunity to examine the rationale for mainstreaming, productive alternatives for mainstreaming program development, and pitfalls that could jeopardize the educational integrity of the classroom and compromise the educational experience of our children.

REFERENCES

Bandura, A. *Aggression: A Social Learning Analysis*. Englewood Cliffs, N.J.: Prentice-Hall, 1973.

Bower, E. M.; Tashnovian, C. A.; and Larson, C. A. "A Process for Early Identification of Emotionally Disturbed Children." Sacramento: California State Department of Education, 1958.

Deno, E. H., ed., *Instructional Alternatives for Exceptional Children*. Reston, Va.: Council for Exceptional Children, no date.

Dunn, L. M. "Special Education for the Mildly Retarded—Is Much of It Justifiable?" *Exceptional Children* 34 (1968): 5–22.

Hewett, F. M. *The Emotionally Disturbed Child in the Classroom*. Boston: Allyn & Bacon, 1968.

Inskeep, Anne D. *Teaching Dull and Retarded Children*. New York: Macmillan, 1926.

Johnson, G. O. "Special Education for the Mentally Handicapped—A Paradox." *Exceptional Children* 29 (1962): 62–69.

———. "Paradox in Special Education—A Reply." *Exceptional Children* 31 (1964): 68–70.

Laing, R. D. *The Politics of Experience*. New York: Pantheon, 1967.

Pappanikou, A. J., and Johnson, A. "The Relationship among Academics, Disturbed, and Disturbing Behavior." Unpublished mimeographed manuscript. Storrs, Ct.: University of Connecticut, 1974.

Redl, F., and Wattenberg, W. *Mental Hygiene in Teaching*. New York: Harcourt, Brace & World, 1959.

Reynolds, M. C., and David, M. D., eds. *Exceptional Children in Regular Classrooms*. Minneapolis: University of Minnesota Leadership Training Institute/Special Education, no date.

Steigman, M. J. "Paradox in Special Education—A Critique of Johnson's Paper." *Exceptional Children* 31 (1964):67–68.

Warfield, G. J., ed. *Mainstream Currents—Reprints from Exceptional Children, 1968–1974*. Reston, Va.: Council for Exceptional Children, 1974.

Mainstreaming Emotionally Disturbed Children

Mainstreaming
Emotionally Disturbed Children

JAMES L. PAUL

OVERVIEW OF MAINSTREAMING

MAINSTREAMING IS ONE among several new catchwords in education. It has become a part of the language of education in the seventies that symbolizes commitments and conflicts spawned during the accelerated development of human services in the sixties.

Mainstreaming has no specific technical meaning, but it has profound implications for the technical business of education. It has social and political meanings which must be fully appreciated and understood if the technical problems are to be solved with any satisfaction.

Mainstreaming emotionally disturbed children involves both the generic issues related to integrating handicapped children and those primarily related to emotional disturbance. Emotionally disturbed children are handicapped and have in common with other handicapped children at least the fact that they have been identified, labeled, and thus singled out as needing special services. Belonging to a group of handicapped children, they share in both the opportunities and problems created by institutional policies and practices. Additionally, however, the emotionally disturbed have been identified as a special group of handicapped children whose handicap has a particular history and social significance to the institution.

The purpose of the present chapter is to provide a general conceptual framework for the book. We shall present three general propositions. First, the historical perspective of mainstreaming, especially the last fifteen years, is an important source of information in understanding mainstreaming. Second, mainstreaming must be understood within the political and philosophical contexts in which it is being developed and promoted. Third, the emotionally disturbed child is perhaps uniquely vulnerable if mainstreaming is not carefully considered and implemented.

Mainstreaming, if taken in its narrowest sense of moving children from special classes to regular classes, raises some very basic questions. The first is, what is right to do, or what is preferred to serve the child's best educational interest? As Turnbull points out in chapter 4 the issues are not entirely clear within a legal framework. We are still dealing more with a matter of policy and preference than with a legal mandate. There is, of course, the very serious risk that the courts, legislators, educators, parents, and others involved in developing institutional law, policy, or procedures could lose perspective on the implications of mainstreaming and create a tidal wave of changes along with an accompanying undesirable institutional undertow. That is, mainstreaming could result in an even less desirable educational arrangement for children if it is implemented without some understanding of the larger social, political, and educational implications.

Parents are sensitive to this possibility. Many parents of handicapped children are now appropriately concerned about mainstreaming. What they fear is that their child will be placed in a situation where success will not be possible and the psychologically defeating failure in educational tasks and in peer interactions will ultimately result in the child's extrusion from school. They fear their child will be "set up" for failure and allow the institutional gears of schools to reclaim the ground parents have fought so hard to win for their children. The question of how best to proceed in mainstreaming children is related to the matter of what constitutes a good education for the handicapped child. This, of course, is part of the larger question of what is quality education. The very powerful movement to establish the right of all children to an education was not directed only at access to the regular classroom.

Teachers also fear mainstreaming as defined in its narrowest sense. They fear behavior they cannot control which will in turn further jeopardize the already tenuous hold they now have on discipline in the classroom. Teachers fear, or resent, being set up for failure themselves. Teachers have a need to achieve and to be successful in their work, teaching. They know there are already children in their classrooms whose educational needs are not being met. Many of them are very concerned about adding to this list.

Both teachers and parents know about the general conclusions reached as a result of the myriad of efficacy studies conducted in the late fifties and early to mid-sixties. They generally know about the legal problem of tracking, Skelley-Wright having become a part of the vernacular of education. They are aware of the general problem of testing and labeling. What they fear, however, is that these and other issues have been built into a Trojan Horse. Many teachers are concerned that the mainstreaming movement will backfire for both the children and the system and further reduce the quality of an already seriously compromised education for all children, including the handicapped.

Mainstreaming presents difficult psychological and sociological problems, including the way we deal with cultural pluralism. Do we seek to reduce diversity through our educational practices? Or, do we wish to increase and affirm those differences? The problems are not solved by simply adding children who add more differences to the regular classroom *if* the educational model and resources in the regular classroom remain the same. This increases the complexity of the educational task for the teacher and further compromises the potential of the regular classroom to be a viable learning environment.

Some have suggested that the education of emotionally disturbed children emerged as a professional area in the sixties as an attempt to reduce the behavioral variation and tension in classrooms. They have viewed the source of those tensions more in the values and cultural differences between children and in unworkable educational philosophies and practices than in psychological disorders. Lewis has, for example, questioned the existence of emotional disturbance. Rhodes has pointed out the cultural residue that collects on the concept of emotional disturbance and the institutional treatment of it. In 1968 the Council for Children with Behavior Disorders meeting in Denver, Colorado, noted the potential of special education as an institutional façade to legitimize racial segregation.

There is, of course, some interaction of the handicapping characteristics of an individual child and the characteristics of an educational system. We may not have sufficiently appreciated the power of the system in that interaction when we were identifying, labeling, and placing the child for what was considered to be "his" problems. Many of the children who become labeled and placed as emotionally disturbed are victims of this very dilemma. Mainstreaming has to develop the assurance it will not further victimize the child who has already demonstrated marginal ability to cope and whose cultural as well as psychological differences have already triggered the extrusion machinery of regular classes.

To summarize, there are many important issues involved in mainstreaming related to education, deviance, and legal as well as human rights. These issues point us to needs unmet, to social and technical problems not yet solved, and to commitments to the handicapped we as a society, and we as professionals have not kept.

DEFINITIONS

Mainstreaming has emerged primarily in relation to the rights of mildly and moderately retarded children to equal educational opportunity. Chaffin (1974) has suggested that the current emphasis on "mainstreaming" the retarded has evolved largely in response to the following: (1) equivocal results of efficacy studies of special classes; (2) inappropriate placement of children in classes for the retarded as a result of the cultural bias of many diagnostic instruments for identifying the retarded; (3) recognizing the debilitating effects of labeling a child; and (4) litigation related to placement procedures and the right of all children to education.

Chaffin has defined mainstreaming as an alternative educational program "characterized by the retention of the mildly retarded child in the regular education classroom with supplemental support being provided to the regular classroom teacher." Chaffin reviewed four models proposed by Deno (1970), Lilly (1970), Gallagher (1972), and Adamson and Van Etten (1972) as alternative delivery systems which, he notes, resulted from Dunn's (1968) critique of special classes for the retarded. The models include more than just alternatives for retarded children. The emphasis in mainstreaming, however, has been primarily on the mentally retarded.

Definitions of mainstreaming have suggested several important dimensions. Rhodes, in Chapter 3, views mainstreaming as a positive slogan expressing social hope in institutional change: "We seem to be borne upon a rising tide of good will toward our fellowman, and to be searching for ways out of a felt impasse in the arena of human care." Turnbull, in Chapter 4, from a legalistic perspective, views mainstreaming as a legislative and judicial preference, more a matter of educational and legal policy and guides to conduct than inflexible rules of conduct. The central issue, as Turnbull indicates, has to do with balancing the interests of children and schools. Pappanikou, Kochanek, and Reich (1974) described mainstreaming as part of special education's search for new models. They point out the recent emphasis on "different environmental approaches to the prevention and amelioration of handicapping conditions in children, which focus on minimizing the stigma and maximizing the handicapped individual's social contact and affiliation with 'normal' role models." They noted that normalization models often preclude special class placement. They proposed a view of special education which facilitates an integrative approach. Their system includes five levels of service, the focus being on continuity, the *raison d'être* of mainstreaming.

There is increasing appreciation of the fact that mainstreaming has important psychological and educational implications for all children, both those who normally make up the mainstream and all of those being brought in. There is increasing concern with the matter of definition and, again, with sorting. Who should be mainstreamed? While it is clear that, from either a psychological or an educational point of view, mainstreaming is not for all children, by what criteria is the decision to be made? This is an especially complex issue for the emotionally disturbed because of the nature of disturbance. There is more standard measurement available for the mentally retarded, for example, than for the emotionally disturbed.

In addition to the criteria for decisions, the way decisions are made and by whom is of major importance. These issues relate to the other edge of mainstreaming. The system must be mainstreamed if handicapped children are to be better served educationally. The decision-making process, who participates in it and how, is an essential feature of the school's accountability structure. Mainstreaming, appropriately understood, can be viewed as a reform of accountability in schools in which the educational arrangement is made more responsive and thus more accountable to the educational interest of all children.

HISTORY

The sixties provided the social and political nourishment for several themes in the evolution of the professionalized and industrialized caregiving. Not all of those themes were compatible. Some were frankly antagonistic.

Prior to the sixties there had existed the we-they institutional dynamic and language that kept patients, residents, and clients away or separated from staff or professionals. The history of the mental health movement tells this story in terms of the culture of hospitals and clinics. There are similarities in the social structure of education with students and teachers. Goffman, Szasz, Blatt, H. Green, and Kesey have helped us appreciate the compromised and often demeaned role of patients and residents. Holt, Kozol, and others have similarly questioned the institutionalized role and status of students. They were among the "radical" voices in the sixties, advocating reform of the institutional arrangements and processes.

There has been movement, especially in the mid to late sixties and early seventies, to try to reestablish the human quality of "institution-bound" relationships. This has included attempts to humanize the educational process, to destigmatize institutional procedures, language, and placement, and to deinstitutionalize those detained or incarcerated in isolated and self-contained settings. There has been a focus on the rights of the person in contrast to the prior focus on the characteristics of the person. Attention to psychopathology gave way to more focus on learning characteristics in the mid to late sixties. The seventies shifted to a focus on rights of children as students, learners, and persons. These shifts were obviously not absolute but rather a matter of relative importance or priority in the attention paid to them. The shifts were the result of several phenomena, including a changing conception of deviance and intervention. They were also the result of a more activist attitude in schools and the helping professions. Advocacy gained traction at this time with the report of the Joint Commission on the Mental Health of Children (1969). Interest in technical programs was not lost but they were now required to share center stage with the rights-oriented advocacy movement which focused more on accountability. Monitoring child environments was a part of this thrust, and it introduced systems technology more broadly to the helping systems. Litigative activity increased to force certain aspects of accountability.

The early seventies have seen the "child servers" and the "child savers" come closer together, both philosophically and conceptually. There has been some blending of interests and perceptions. Both fear the loss of control in making sound program decisions. Some of the trust barriers have been transcended.

One of the most important developments in this regard resulted from the increase in massive human service bureaucracies in the sixties. Coupled with the bureaucracy in education, this became an increasingly oppressive force and made rational planning more and more difficult. Early in the accountability movement of the sixties the problem was thought of in terms of ill-willed or incompetent people. Now there has been more acceptance of the view that the advocates and the professionals have a common enemy in the unresponsive and ineffective aspects of bureaucracies of child-serving systems. It is in this regard that, for example, the largness of institutions is recognized in *Futures of Children* as a major problem in its own right. Bureaucracy inhibits both human caring and technical functions.

The essential point that must be made in considering shifts of focus has to do with balance. There is the risk of exaggerated responses to narrowness, incompleteness or even error in the system when it is "discovered" or more fully or publicly appreciated. Mainstreaming runs the risk of shortsighted over-reaction to weaknesses in our current system of educating handicapped children. The problems of over-reaction include institutionalized "solutions" to the wrong problems and the development of laws that are as inadequate as those we have now.

THE NEED FOR CHANGE

There has been an historic tendency for public school bureaucracy to incorporate manifestations or artifacts of educational ideas and to fail to generate the essential policies, professional competencies, and attitudes to support and maintain the viability of those innovations. Special classes are, in many instances, examples of maintaining the institutional form in the absence of the educational idea. In many instances special classes have become places of exile, philosophically detached from the regular education program. Discontinuity of curriculum between the special and regular classroom sets up the condition for separate and, frequently, unequal education.

Mainstreaming should not result in the dismantling of special classes as long as there are children who need an educational program that can best be provided in that setting. Since there are still some children who can best be served in special classes, these settings must be maintained. They should be dismantled when—and only when—we have the ability to provide a better education for all children without special classes.

What is needed is not to remove or dismantle the artifact, the special setting, but to provide the reform necessary to reconstitute the idea of continuity of educational support for all children. Such reform should avoid the trappings of faddism. Special classes became fads. A counter-fad under the banner of mainstreaming can hardly be reassuring to parents, children, or teachers either in the mainstream of education or its tributaries.

No one has provided a convincing blueprint for revitalizing the total system of education, and, as already suggested, it is that total system that is involved when we consider the mainstream. The total educational establishment is bursting at its bureaucratic seams with problems in collective bargaining with teachers' unions, with logistics of mass transportation of children, and with programs of behavior control. Some want to burn and bury it. Others want to reform it. Attacked both for what it does wrongly, such as labeling children, and for what it fails to do, such as providing all children an education, the public school continues as the primary institutional system for the public education of children. It is a reality. Mainstreaming calls attention to both the sanity and the sickness in school and society and the relationship between them.

That scope, however, should not blind us to the possibilities of professional reform at the level of the handicapped child's interactions with the system as well as at the organizational and policy level. Mainstreaming should promote the freeing of handicapped children from any procedure or setting which limits their educational experience. Abusive classification of children should be as much a target of the freeing impulse of mainstreaming as special class placement. Both inappropriate labeling and placement of a child compromise the integrity and freedom of the child.

There are sources of guidance in approaching this complex problem. The report of the Project on Classification of Exceptional Children (Hobbs 1974), for example, provides an excellent analysis of the issues and makes recommendations for reducing the problem. This material provides helpful information for thinking about standards for what is and is not acceptable in certain institutionalized practices with children.

EMOTIONAL DISTURBANCE IN SCHOOLS: HISTORICAL PERSPECTIVE

The following discussion focuses more specifically on emotionally disturbed children and the implications of mainstreaming for their education.

In the sixties the emotionally disturbed child, as a matter of social policy, gained a right to an education. Before the sixties there was no major support in public schools for emotionally disturbed children. These children had been educationally ignored in the regular classroom if their behavior was compliant, left in psychiatric hospitals often because there was no appropriate educational program in the schools, misplaced in classes for the retarded, or excluded from school altogether because of behavior problems and the school's inability to cope with or respond to their needs.

When the emotionally disturbed child did receive services, it was under special circumstances. Other handicapped children in the past had been provided an altered educational curriculum or had been provided with prosthetic assistance to circumvent their disability. The emotionally disturbed child, however, as Trippe (1963) pointed out, was expected to change to meet the requirements of an unmodified regular education curriculum.

This child did not have a disability which teachers, parents, and friends could see and recognize as limiting his ability to function. There was no test he could take that would render an "emotional disturbance quotient" that would produce a classification and cause him to be viewed as handicapped. This was, of course, not all bad. It did, however, contribute to the condition in which disturbance became synonymous with difference, and, when the term gained popular usage, it became a way for teachers to rationalize their lack of response to his educational needs: "He's disturbed, I can't teach him." Or, "Since I cannot teach him and he has no other handicap, he must be disturbed." Manifestations of this child's handicap were more likely to stimulate negative affect—anger, fear, and rejection—than feelings of concern and a wish to help.

The sixties, however, did identify the emotionally disturbed child as needing educational services and established his right as a handicapped child to have special education services. In addition, a number of significant developments occurred which had positive implications for services affecting the emotionally disturbed child: legislative and economic support was generated; public attitudes became more supportive; a professional work force, utilizing an improved and more efficient methodology, especially in the application of behavioral principles, was developed; and alternative organizational arrangements both within the public schools and between schools and other child-serving systems were implemented.

One of the major debates of the sixties concerning the emotionally disturbed child had to do with the way the phenomenon of disturbance would be viewed and who would have ultimate professional dominion over the philosophy and practice of educating emotionally disturbed children. It was within this general context that the so-called medical model was examined—primarily a political issue having to do with professional and institutional authority. There was a major problem, however, in definition.

Part of the issue of defining emotional disturbance had to do with finding a way to look at the problem that would fit available educational procedures and arrangements for responding appropriately. Educators had to get a handle on the phenomenon for which they were assuming responsibility. Psychology was very accommodating.

Some fields of psychology fully appreciate the tenuous phenomenology of mental illness. Some conceptual "handles" on the activity of animals had been generated in experimental laboratories which provided a springboard for behavioral psychology to move into the conceptual and methodological vacuum involved in "educating" emotionally disturbed children. It framed a way to define the problems of emotional disturbance as well as an approach to curriculum planning. Many special classes became behavior laboratories where behavioral procedures could be learned and practiced. The procedures received more attention than the places where they were practiced. The process involved in obtaining desired behavior was of more direct concern than the desired behavior or goals.

The social phenomenology of emotional disturbance was, for the most part, lost to the science of behavior analysis and change. Educators and psychologists, who were not exclusively oriented to a psychodynamic point of view, became so involved in the application of successful behavioral procedures that many allowed the social meaning and ethics of intervention to be minimized as a significant issue.

Both the personal appeal of social exchange theory and the power of the medical establishment in defining the problem psychiatrically, however, helped maintain an argument that provided a balancing perspective. That argument has been facilitated by professional, social, legal, and legislative events of the late sixties and early seventies. While the issues that emerged in the sixties were never totally resolved—there are philosophical and institutional remnants of old battles—the seventies are producing new issues which need the perspective of the sixties.

EMERGING THEMES AND EDUCATIONAL PROBLEMS

While it would not be relevant here to deal extensively with the trends in educating emotionally disturbed children, some are directly or indirectly related to mainstreaming emotionally disturbed children or our think-ing about emotional disturbance. Some of the issues or emerging themes and certain educational problems involved will be discussed here briefly.

Theories of disturbance have been studied in their own right with the hope, among other things, of finding some unifying perspective or synthesis of the various theories used to explain and/or describe dis-turbance (Rhodes and Tracy 1972). While the study organized knowl-edge of theory, there was no organizing framework found or developed to bring the various viewpoints into a single perspective. Several things can now be said, however, about where we are in relation to theory. First, there is no longer the singular preoccupation with psychodynamic models as was the case in the early sixties. Second, there is not the magical expectations of behavioral methodologies that existed in the late sixties. Third, several viewpoints have been programmatically incorpor-ated by most professionals rather than relying exclusively on one. Fourth, there has been more focus on the adaptive behavior of the child in relation to the characteristics of environments in which adaptation is expected (Rhodes 1973). There has been less attention given to blame or causality and more attention given to interaction. Consequently, there has been more concern for alternative support systems and environments. This has included increased organizational flexibility and curriculum reform. The engineered classroom, or, as Hewett would now prefer, the "orchestrated" classroom, is an excellent example. There has been an increased concern with the delivery system. The bureaucratization of services has become more a matter of direct concern where intractable institutional procedures compromise the fairness, reasonableness, and professional wisdom with which a child is handled. Institutionalization is being vigorously resisted, and deinstitutionalization activity has con-siderable support—both in terms of a person's right to live in or as close to his community as possible and the least freedom-limiting alternative intervention.

In the seventies it has become no longer sufficient to be successful; one must also be humane. The rites of science are being challenged by the right of persons. Preoccupation with technical accuracy is being challenged by a concern with moral rightness. This challenge gained its most substantial traction when being wrong became, through litigation based on constitutional claims, the equivalent of being illegal. Educa-tional practices, particularly the failure to provide appropriate educa-tional services, are now being examined and judged by constitutional standards. It is not enough to provide a place for the disabled in an in-stitution—he has a right to treatment. It is no longer acceptable to say the child is not entitled to be educated because he cannot be taught—he has a right to an appropriate education. Educational arrangements found to be not very educative have been examined for their social "costs" to students. The emotionally disturbed child—understood by many educators a decade earlier as behaviorally discordant, a victim of bad habits, a child whose behavior exceeded the tolerance thresholds of the environments in which he was identified as disturbing, and, later, a violator of social rules and contracts—now arguably inherits at least part of the constitutional cloak of citizen.

The situation is difficult at best. The cultural center for all children is guaranteed by social arrangement and by law to be the public school. At its center is a scandal. Schools are citizenmakers. Yet schools have been found guilty of segregating and stigmatizing the disturbed and other handicapped children, frequently under the guise of scientific practice. Some have pointed out that schools provide, in many instances, a concentration of social pathology and citizen-alien models of behavior and values.

Educators are caught again with a mandate they are at odds to fill—that is, righting social and sometimes constitutional wrongs within the framework of educational practices. This is further complicated by the fact that schools have become big bureaucracies with such features of big business as collective bargaining and teachers' unions. Where do the teachers' rights end and the children's rights begin, and vice versa? This was not a major problem when the teacher ruled unquestioned over her charges and there was a continuity of values between teachers and parents and children in the classroom. It becomes a problem when the discontinuity is so basic that judicial involvement is necessary and when adults other than the teachers, including parents, have to become more significantly involved in the educational decision-making process as advocates for their children. This is the context in which mainstreaming is evolving as a new thrust in education. The waters of the mainstream and the tributaries are troubled.

In summary, then, emotionally disturbed children have obtained a place in the educational system since the early sixties, and, increasingly, a program that responds to their needs. These children have been especially vulnerable to the behavioral requirements of the regular classroom. They are prime candidates for all punitive potential in a classroom. Most of these children are in the mainstream but not necessarily of, or supported by, the mainstream. Children who are in special classes and could profit more from an instructional program in the regular classroom should be moved to the regular classroom with the necessary supportive services to make that adaptation successful. Some emotionally disturbed children, however, are as close in special classes to the mainstream as they can be at this time and still have an opportunity to succeed as students. Their place must also be protected. Those children who are in public school special classes who otherwise would be in a psychiatric hospital are—most likely by their perception and that of their parents—in the mainstream.

COUNTER THEMES IN THE EDUCATION OF THE EMOTIONALLY DISTURBED

More radical themes are being developed that interact directly with the idea of mainstreaming emotionally disturbed children. One is that the whole concept of normality or normness implies a common reality. Differences, in the past dealt with as negative deviation resulting from personal incompetence or disorder, may be more a different reality to be understood than the negative end of a social behavior scale. Apart from our expectations, we do not assess difference and, apart from our evaluation, difference may not be bad. Emotional disturbance, perhaps more than any other handicap, interacts with the personal values of those who define it. Emotional disturbance, as suggested earlier, may label our negative evaluation of much of the residue of cultural differences in the public schools.

Another theme has to do with caring. Caretaking has been institutionalized and, thus, depersonalized. There is a move to reexamine relationships and put them in a context of mutual subjectivity. The persons of the caring and the cared for are involved. The scientific cloak of objectivity is being reexamined and found to be brittle in human relationships. While objectivity facilitates the development of one domain of knowledge, it leaves out much that is the human experience. What I do can be described, counted, compared. How I "fit," connect, relate (we do not have a good vocabulary for it) with you is a part of the experience we share. That experience is the essence of me, of who I am. Who I am cannot be reduced to what I do.

The increasing definition of human relationships and problems in living in objective terms reached a significant crescendo in the sixties. Behaviorism, narrowly conceived, revived the fantasy and provided the hope, again, that with "scientific" management there was the possibility of eliminating deviance and mental illness, reminiscent of the late 1800s with the advances in topographical neurology (Hart 1931). The good life could be shaped. That hope was played out very briefly in the public schools.

Very interesting philosophical shifts in direction emerged. For some time it was the synthesis of the several intervention methodologies into a more creditable program. Even the new eclectics, however, have continued to concern themselves primarily with methodology and intervention process.

There has been an expanding minority concerned with goals and with the view of man manifested in professional and institutional practices. The questions of this group are not confined to traditional boundaries of validity, reliability, and efficiency of intervention. Their concern has resurrected questions that, historically, pre-date the new "science" of treatment. Their questions are more: What right do we have to intervene; who am I to intervene; and what is better (goals) for the person that would guide the changes I seek? These are ethical questions and require examination of basic assumptions. They invite the subjective into center court, very different from the attitude that sees the subjective as the source of distortion. The individual's reality becomes more important than universal law. Difference may be instructive, it may be better, and thus, should be listened to for its potential wisdom rather than isolated, identified as a problem, and controlled.

Laing (1967) and others have led us into a reconsideration of individual human experience and the nature of that reality. Rhodes has helped focus attention on the value of difference. He speaks of personal joy and the celebration of deviance. He goes further to suggest that what is celebrated is the reviving undercurrents of caring, deep in individual experience. Celebration is for the discovery of life in ourselves, of communion in finding life in others. Joy is in affirming life and its value. It is in the reassurance of our capacity to transcend our professional and bureaucratized conceptions of ourselves and the other. This language is more comfortably fitted into poetry or religion than the formal concerns of pedagogy or psychology.

Seeley (1952) has provided us with an excellent review of how the mental health movement moved into the power vacuum created by the decline of the church. The language was changed but much of the form was maintained. The sixties saw the mental health movement absorbed into the public schools. Some spoke of schools as the preferred mental health center (Stickney 1968). This further comingled the mental health business with the cultural mainstream and society's work in the socialization of children. This has stimulated some reassessment of both mental health and education.

The "radical" forces do not have a well-developed methodology. What they require is commitment and, for some, a change in life style. The political power and the impact of existentialism as a philosophy was limited in the late fifties and early sixties because it did not include a prescription for behavior. It provided a language and a way of thinking about individual experience that probed the heart of the mental health movement. Much of the current resistance to the formal views of mental illness and the institutional practices of mental health, including the practices in schools, are the flowering of doubts and alternative possibilities planted by existentialism in the late fifties and early sixties.

CONCLUDING STATEMENT

It is dangerous to proceed with only a navigational target, a sense of direction and goals, or with only maps and technical equipment for travel, i.e., a methodology. There must be a balance of perspective, credible goals, and some ability to move in the direction they suggest. The curriculum, as Hewitt argues, must include attention to what is to be taught, the behaviors expected, as well as what one does if the behavior does not occur. If there must be legislative prodding to accomplish mainstreaming in the sense of increasing options for children, affirming the value of diversity, including opening the doors to special classes and swinging them in both directions, there must be: (1) a careful consideration of what the educational system ought to be (goals); (2) standards for acceptable procedures; (3) a viable public-involving system to determine those goals and standards, as well as to monitor and enforce them; and (4) vigorous effort to make the most sophisticated and credible technical resources effectively and efficiently available to those who work with children on the goals.

In later chapters, Whelan, Hewett, and Fink suggest some ways to get at the different aspects of the problem. Pappanikou describes one way to get at mainstreaming the system. Turnbull reminds us that mainstreaming as an intervention has profound impact on children and their families as well as the schools, and that we proceed in a context of law which, while not articulated in any detail relative to the issues of mainstreaming emotionally disturbed children, does assure certain rights and protections. While being held accountable within a judicial framework, we have tremendous opportunity and responsibility to influence the legislative framework.

Martin (1974) has provided a sobering statement warning us of the consequences for children if we, as a professional area, indulge ourselves in mainstreaming children without proper planning and careful attention to the issues involved. Special education has a history and, for all its malpractice, that history is a source of wisdom for improving our services to handicapped children. There are many proposals for improving the education of handicapped children including eliminating special education as a separate area of education. There are many new possibilities for becoming more responsible advocates for handicapped children. To be inactive is to encourage the possibility of the artifacts of special education, including those we value least, becoming more common practice—the basis for policy formulation and for new law.

What is presented in this book is not an answer to the questions raised here, but a discussion of the complexity of several dimensions of mainstreaming emotionally disturbed children. It is an attempt to stimulate more discussion of the issues and hopefully contribute to a more reasonable and reasoned approach to mainstreaming.

The chapters that follow attempt to deal philosophically, conceptually, and to some extent, organizationally and programatically with mainstreaming emotionally disturbed children. Mainstreaming is viewed as a complex issue which raises both important philosophical and technical questions. It is considered as part of a larger movement to reform or transform the special education of handicapped children. It is suggested that, like other large, institutional, change-oriented movements, mainstreaming needs to be encouraged with caution lest we create even more serious problems for the children. The general position taken is that the system must be mainstreamed, as well as the children. Each of the chapters that follow deals with some aspect of mainstreaming which contributes to one or more of these conclusions.

REFERENCES

Adamson, G., and Van Etten, G. "Zero Reject Model Revisited: A Workable Alternative." *Exceptional Children* (1972): 38.

Blatt, B., and Kaplan, F. *Christmas in Purgatory.* Syracuse: Human Policy Press, 1965.

Chaffin, J. D. "Will the Real 'Mainstreaming' Program Please Stand Up!" *Focus on Exceptional Children* (1974): 6.

Crisis in Child Mental Health: Challenge for the 1970's. Joint Commission on the Mental Health of Children. New York: Harper and Row, 1970.

Deno, E. "Special Education as Developmental Capital." *Exceptional Children* (1970): 37.

Dunn, L. M. "Special Education for the Mildly Retarded: Is Much of It Justifiable?" *Exceptional Children* (1968): 35.

Gallagher, J. J. "The Special Education Contract for Mildly Handicapped Children." *Exceptional Children* (1972): 38.

Goffman, E. *Asylums*. Garden City, N.Y.: Anchor, 1961.

Green, H. *I Never Promised You a Rose Garden*. New York: Signet, 1964.

Hart, Bernard. *The Psychology of Insanity*. 4th ed. New York: Macmillan, 1939.

Hobbs, Nicholas. *The Futures of Children*. San Francisco: Jossey-Bass, 1975.

Holt, J. *How Children Fail*. New York: Dell, 1964.

Kesey, K. *One Flew Over the Cuckoo's Nest*. New York: Viking, 1962.

Kozol, J. *Death at an Early Age*. Boston: Houghton Mifflin, 1967.

Laing, R. D. *The Politics of Experience*. New York: Ballantine, 1967.

Lilly, S. M. "Special Education: A Teapot in a Tempest." *Exceptional Children* (1970): 37.

Martin, Edwin W. "Some Thoughts on Mainstreaming." *Exceptional Children* 41 (3) (November 1974): 150–53.

Pappanikou, A. J., Kochanek, T. T., and Reich, M. L. "Continuity and Unity in Special Education." *Phi Delta Kappan* 55 (8) (1974).

Rhodes, William C., and Tracy, M. L. *A Study of Child Variance: Conceptual Project in Emotional Disturbance*. Vol. 1. Ann Arbor, Mich.: University of Michigan Press, 1972.

Seeley, John R. "Social Values, The Mental Health Movement and Mental Health." *Annals of the American Academy of Political and Social Science* 286 (March 1953): 15–24.

Stickney, Stonewall. "Mental Health in the Schools." Unpublished John Umstead Lecture. Raleigh, N.C.: State Department of Mental Health, 1968.

Szasz, T. *The Myth of Mental Illness*. New York: Dell, 1967.

Trippe, M. "Conceptual Problems in Research on Educational Provisions for Disturbed Children." *Exceptional Children* 29 (1963): 400–406.

2

The Psychology of Mainstreaming
Socio-Emotionally Disturbed Children

WILLIAM C. MORSE

T HE CONCEPT AND PROMISE of mainstreaming for the socio-emotionally disturbed can be considered from diverse viewpoints. Historically it is nothing new: old style mainstreaming was once the total
program and still is all that has been provided for many special education pupils. Politically, mainstreaming has been a popular approach and
is envisioned as a way to serve more with less during this period of acute
financial stress. A pupil is hardly special except for brief encounters
and this has already led to the idea that reimbursement should be on a
piecework basis—the child being special only when not in the mainstream. Administratively, mainstreaming might look simple at first
glance, and consultation avoids the accountability and responsibility
which accompanies direct service to children. In many districts the
teachers and their unions are not yet aware of the meaning of the new
design. Regular teachers themselves frequently express dismay when
they learn of the new obligations and extended accountability they have
inherited.

Mainstreaming is usually combined with mandatory legislation
giving parents and advocates a new power base for participation in getting service for children in need. Special education professionals range
in opinion about mainstreaming from seeing it as a loss of financial and
operational control to helping children to the dawn of the new day
when special education is about to direct and reform the total educational establishment. Whether the specialists will actually increase or decrease their influence is still an interesting speculation. Philosophically

18

we cannot forget that whatever actually happens in given circumstances, mainstreaming is the hope for a more humane and concerned special education. The guilt for our past sins and the cultural revolution leads us to know we must learn to do better. All of these pieces of the mosaic are deserving of the attention given them in the various chapters in this volume.

But attention to these matters does not allow us to avoid the central purpose of it all. The psychological study of mainstreaming focuses on one issue: how well does this process provide the actual experiences which the socio-emotionally deviant pupil needs? This psychological examination starts with the definition of our special education pupils. The socio-emotionally disturbed pupils are those, who by virtue of the dissonance pervading their inner and outer life space, have a need for more intense and more sophisticated professional investment than do their normal peers. The simple fact is, if there is no need for this special input, the youngster should not be considered a special education pupil. The unsimple fact is, if he has special needs, we have not yet begun the proper examination of how we can actually provide the help. The preoccupation with the various mechanics of the delivery of service is better suited to milk distribution than to providing mental health. It puts emphasis more on the conceptual efficiency of a system than on the profound complications inherent in re-raising a child who is in the midst of his own unique constellation of stress. This is a psychological problem.

EXPLORING THE PSYCHOLOGICAL NATURE OF OUR TASK

We may begin our psychological exploration by reminding ourselves of an assumption. This assumption is that most of our subset population of special education, in contrast to other areas, can be restored and made whole. This goal of normality or recoverability sets off a chain of accountability expectations seldom recognized. Some have a goal of more than normality for these deviant pupils: they anticipate a high level of self-actualization. There is also the confounding aspect that the child's normal developmental growth is destined to produce periods of relative stress and relief within and without. This flux must be separated from long-term directional change. Since in many states special education resources are not legally available for prevention or crisis, the problem has to reach a proven "bad" level before it is "good" enough to be serviced. Without the continua of mental health service, the uncategorized child or adolescent is left to his own devices since he is not ours. We speak of alternative plans for such special program mismatches, but we forget that the intensity of help required may be equal, though presumably for a shorter time span.

But there are other matters. From the ecological point of view espoused by Rhodes (1970), we know we must be equally concerned with the child's nature and milieu factors. This expands the universe of both assessment and interventions. Again, since socio-emotional problems are seldom found in a pristine state, we should be involved with the welfare of special pupils who may "belong" to some other label, though they may have an overlay of emotional difficulty. Finally, we are given to ignore the fact that many of the socio-economical problems are not born of the educational enterprise (though some are and others may be exacerbated by the school). But the necessary interventions may not be primarily educational in the usual school sense. It is not uncommon to see special programs for socio-emotionally impaired pupils which do not have even a remote mental health component.

It is necessary to devote brief attention to the children included before moving to specific psychological aspects of mainstreaming. Though special education has persisted in picking and choosing what it would consider, there are three syndromes which are included. Since these have been described in detail (Morse in Cruickshank 1975 and Morse 1975), we need only to make it clear that we are not speaking of minor or temporary defections of behavior where cures are simple and even instant. While the fact is that the individual profile overrides any general pattern, the meaning of the child's specific symptoms rests in the pattern. Regardless of how the impairments were generated or the theories about recovery, there are three general states of serious impairment. The first overall pattern stems from an incapacitating struggle between impulse and control. At a conscious or unconscious level there will be evidence of subjective distress, anxiety, and guilt. Such children may act out or be depressed and are usually plagued by severely damaged self-esteem. A second category, which has often been ignored by special education, consists of children and youth who are growing up with serious defects in socialization. These are the value-deficient (as contrasted with value-different) children who are growing up without acquiring an age-appropriate concern for others. This pattern is probably the most rapidly growing group; we also see an increasing number of girls who evidence this dilemma. As the primary socialization factors in society have become less effective, there are more and more desperate children with no trust and no caring, who live on their impulses. They are damaged both by blunted feelings for others and by their limitations in using symbols, or reading (King 1975 and 1976). Third, special education is responsible for the severely disabled children who have profound communication difficulties, acute relationship distortions, and difficulty coping with even a simplified environment. They seem to have no interest in others and live immersed in their own preoccupations; their play produces neither the normal exploration nor the satisfaction found in the normal youngster. While many hold that both psychotic and autistic children have a limited future, we must increase our efforts to help.

Mainstreaming must be put in the context of the psychological nature of those children in the above syndromes. This raises two central considerations. One is that the idiosyncratic nature of each child determines the specific intervention of choice. The behavior patterns which help us think and plan cannot be a substitute for individualization of the work. Just as each child is individual, conversely, there is no mainstream entity. We made that mistake when we created the fiction of a hypothetical special class. We even talked about special classes as if the name delineated a given psychological substance. Let us not make the mistake again. There are as many mainstreams as there are youngsters mainstreamed. Each has a unique set of intervention resources and strictures.

We turn now to a brief examination of the two parts of the puzzle— the children and the mainstream place. What is in the search for the degree of match? At best, we know very little about the children we would serve. Our lack of skill in understanding them has driven us to tests and devices, to meetings and consultations. Anything but the child! It is of much concern to find psychological tests now being given and interpreted by untrained personnel. It is of equal concern to find new unproven devices spawned at every turn. If we have enough scales to depend upon, there is no need to test our human understanding, which is what clinical skill was all about. It would be refreshing to ask, in the midst of the reports of data collected about the child, if the real child would please stand up. Of course he usually could not stand up because he is not really here. We are all busy trying to reconstruct him from examining his artifacts which we have collected. He has become an archeological discovery, known from his remains and not his person. And if he did stand up, would we recognize him? Diagnosis has become the blind foursome who, as the story goes, described their knowledge of the elephant. When we look at the evidence from discussions about disturbed children, we learn as much about the perceiver as the perceived.

The crux of the issue of mainstreaming lies in differential knowl-

86452

edge about the needs of a pupil. There seems to be an illusion that severity is the index of placement. "Mild cases" (whatever they are) can be mainstreamed, while severe ones never can be, or so we are told. Anyone who has tried to work with an ego-intact, value-deviant delinquent in a classroom might decide to try very different and more seriously impaired in the classroom the next time. We have as yet worked out no system for determining who can be helped where.

Since anyone's behavior is always a consequence of a given ratio of the internal and external condition, we can no longer focus on either just the child or just the environment. The diagnostic search is conducted to discover (Morse 1974) which intervention is relevant in the particular child-environment ratio. There is also the danger of the "greenhouse" phenomenon: an environment which exactly meets the needs of the deviant child may create an instant elimination of his reactive behavior, but is this a cure? Some believe that, if the environment is unprovoking, the given child will heal himself. Other times we anticipate that any correctional influence will take time to prepare for the later transplanting out of the greenhouse. Developmental growth counts for something, but we often wonder how much.

On the other hand, mainstreaming might result in a necessary confrontation revealing the child's inability to cope successfully. The problem can then be dealt with realistically. Teaching socio-emotionally impaired children presents a unique and continual challenge whether the pupil is in a special setting or in the mainstream. We want him to work up to his ability, but we do not want to push him beyond his coping capacity. We try to work at the very cutting edge of his cognitive and affective potential. This requires that teachers neither over- nor undersupport the youngster. This is a continual clinical judgment. If we require too little, the child is robbed of his ability to function on his own. If we give too little, we undersupport the need. If we give too much, the child remains dependent on the "helper."

Probably the most significant thing we can hope for in mainstreaming is innovation in the ability to infuse school with interventions (new and old) rather than the illusion of an automatic great stride forward based on the geography of where we put the problem. Often the old classes for the emotionally disturbed did very little for the "statistical average" pupil, but did help some a great deal. It was also clear that special classes so called were often really not special at all (Morse, Cutler, and Fink 1971). At other times and for particular pupils and their families the special class added insult to original injury. Then the task became one of getting the child to quit fighting the delivery system, never getting to his basic problem for which the placement was made. We have yet to study the persons for whom the class is useful versus those for whom it is not. Mainstreaming does not eliminate intervention problems; it just presents a new set of variables—a set, we hope, that can be better managed if we use it for the right youngsters.

Partly because of our educational myopia, we have had a tendency to overlook the psychological needs of the child. As it is put, the diagnosis must be educationally relevant. It can be that and still not relevant to the child we are trying to help. It may be heretical to say that every socio-emotionally disturbed child may not be a special education problem. Of course they must have schooling, and to say that rescue will not come from special education does not mean we should not provide special education. Many of the easy educationally based cures written about are children whose behavior was a consequence of direct educational insult. These are reversible through educational interventions alone if caught soon enough. Not so with the many children who are casualties of massive family and societal destructiveness. The potential for restoration and compensatory support for these children is a matter of a life support system and not a class or a regular classroom alone. The educator who advocates going it alone in such instances will find the well-meaning effort of excellent teachers consumed in the too little which is provided.

With the diminution of multi-disciplined involvement and the ascendance of educational responsibility, we have unwittingly boxed ourselves in. The socio-emotionally disturbed child may not respond to special education. While the school often generates or acerbates a condition, education may be the *major* intervention channel, *one* of the channels, or it may be a *low power* involvement.

EDUCATIONAL PROGRAMS IN PERSPECTIVE

As we examine what is necessary to help a youngster toward a reasonable personal and social life, we have to ask to what degree the total milieu must be controlled and what specialization must be infused in the milieu if we are to be successful. We have to ask what must happen to give the child a new lease on life.

Will changes be necessary in the family and community, or will a change in how the child perceives and responds to the conditions be sufficient? Will minor changes in the child's behavior heal an interactive pattern (Henry 1971)? The work of Love (1974) suggests non-traditional, school-related methods for altering families on the ego level, which may be enough. If one can adjust the curriculum and method and by this end the child's problem, that is one thing. Experience with severe value deviancy raises question about even a total milieu (unless it is highly sophisticated) ever providing what is needed.

When the change is made from providing a program to providing a sufficient program, the situation will be vastly different. To some of us educational accountability has become an excuse by the community for providing for the needs of emotionally and socially deviant children. A school program takes over just a part of life, but it can be made to look as though it cares for all of the child's needs so we can avoid the programs required for a total effort.

The generic problem of providing for the real psychological needs of the child does not change with a special provision or mainstreaming. We never mastered meeting the needs in special classes which is one reason for the mainstream mania. Sometimes, related to the special class, the most incisive experiences were on the bus trips and not in the actual classes at all—so little did we attend to the psychological realities. There are public school programs which have incorporated group therapy, individual therapy, and family interventions. There are those for adolescents which engage in work "therapy" but these are the exception to the rule. Even when resources of the work experience type are available to mainstream adolescents, members of our group are frequently rejected as misfits.

In planning interventions we have been very naive, ignoring the complexity of socio-emotional disturbance. Always we look for a short cut. There are three generalizations which have emerged in my own thinking with regard to this. The first generalization is that the child is a dynamic organism who fortunately often remolds what is done to him to fit his problem even if it is a poor choice. It follows then that there is no one magic way to assist a child. This lack of specificity results in the sometimes success by a wide variety of interventions and, at the same time, the never perfect success by any one mode—be it curriculum or psychotherapy, neither or both. Finkel (1976) lists twenty-two currently practiced approaches to psychotherapy along with six principal group therapies. This listing is really a restricted classical listing of therapy and those of us who have followed Redl see the therapeutic *potential* of many, many more approaches (Morse 1972), most of which can be incorporated into the school experience. Many are emphasized in this volume. Can we professionals live long enough to get over focusing on the delivery mechanic rather than the pupil's problem? If we do begin to appreciate the wide variety of interventions which may be effective, we next realize that our ability to predict which one is appropriate for which youngster is often low. In a way this is because "help" is in the eyes of the helpee, not the helper. It is often indirect rather than direct, and has a quality of the consumer's perception about it.

A second generalization comes from the observation that pilot programs often cannot be considered as pilots at all. The successful model in many cases simply does not transfer. This may be because what is effective in obtaining positive results may not be the thing to which people attribute the change. The Hawthorne effect, zest, deeper human commitment, the hope engendered and caring (expressed in diverse ways to be sure), the emotion of initial surge vs. the grinding long term hauls —things of this nature may be involved. Thus it seems that the covert psychological conditions underlying help may override the overt elements described.

Third, the impatience for instant change looms large. It is possible that this violates the essential nature of child growth, development, and especially remediation. One could almost say if there is instant or rapid change there was either no real problem in the first place or else the new behavior is superficial. Yet impatience about change makes for much false expectation. What we should be concerned with is life stream as a psychological process and what we talk about is mainstreaming as an educational process. The degree to which the mainstreaming mode of instant pressing out of plastic objects in this society has been embraced by the child raisers is an indication of the shallow understanding of children which pervades our work.

The goal then should be to assess (we can no longer talk much about diagnosis) the dissonance in the person and place system as Rhodes has said and then apply the best possible psychological interventions.

ANALYZING THE PSYCHOLOGICAL RESOURCES
IN THE MAINSTREAM

Kendall (1971) was one of the first to discuss the psychological realities of mainstreaming, and he based much of his point of view on the fact that "school systems are notoriously resistant to fundamental change." The questions he raises have to do with the nature of mainstream resources for the special child. These range from curriculum to attitudes, and not one of them is subject to easy control. We can focus on this matter by examining the three main sources of psychological input in the mainstream: the adults, the peers, and the tasks. The utility of mainstreaming has to do with what these immediate sources produce and what the child requires for both maintenance and improvement. The impact must not only be hygienic; it must be restorative. These are the matters which underlie the chapters in the present volume and are conditions which we must learn to understand in full.

The Teacher's Input

It is well known that training and ability have only a low correlation. There are regular teachers who are able to interact usefully with socio-emotionally disturbed children though they never took a course, do not know the terms, and could not describe what they do. But there are also limits (of the initiated and uninitiated as well) in capacity to be psychologically helpful. In mainstreaming we had better seek out the natural human resources in teachers rather than take on the task of making over the whole profession. For example, children who need structure and an adult with a sense of authority should not be put in a classroom where the native style of that teacher does not embody such resources. The consequence of expecting the mainstream agents to generate a scarce or absent psychological input will lead only to defeat. Of course the fact that a pupil is sustained by a teacher does not always mean that there will be any automatic growth to absorb the problem which the child has. When we expect that the teacher or some resource adult will have to help the youngster with profound distortions of feelings, additional skills are needed in the mainstream. Can the teacher counsel in depth with the pupil? Does the teacher have the ability to dissociate counter transference responses? We know that trained and untrained alike falter (King 1976) in handling aggressive behavior which is a major component. Can the teacher referee the psychological games and avoid the traps children play with adults and peers (Newman 1974)? By any stretch of the imagination, can the teacher be a figure to fill the void in the child's identification pattern? From this viewpoint, we must consider the proper use of the native adult resources in the mainstream for the necessary psychological input. Somtimes there will be resources enough and other times not enough.

The Peer Climate

Classroom groups differ significantly in their mental health resource index. There are stable, resilient groups which absorb and diminish the output of a deviant child. Some go further and reach out in an empathic way to help a troubled child. Other groups have such a low margin or are already saturated with problems, whether designated as special education or not, that a precarious, marginal balance can be destroyed with an addition in the mainstream. There are groups with a frustration quotient so high that scapegoating is the order of the day. Other groups have so little reservoir of peer liking that there is no relationship to offer a new pupil. Fearful groups may be traumatized by the behavior of some youngsters. The dynamics of class size in itself is little considered in mainstreaming. The huge class sizes invoked to solve budget problems determine the time teachers have to invest in each pupil. What one pupil gets extra another pupil misses, and sooner or later the majority of the children (or the parents) are going to catch on and object. The "value of learning to live with different children" may not be adequate compensation. At present, the movement to employ aides, get and train volunteers, and other modes to add to the ratio of adult investment is in need of a great deal of study.

It is our observation that the current social disorganization is producing a significant group of children without a primary group experience needed to establish basic trust and a sense of self identity. The usual classroom secondary group will not be enough: in fact such a child will attempt to use the classroom in ways destined to failure. Or to take another problem, current role identification problems of girls are producing an increasing number of failures which will need a more intensive relationship than is possible in many classrooms. If we are going to provide what is needed, we will have to find ways of breaking down the group size without putting expectations on regular classroom teachers which will drive them to further distraction. Let alone solving this problem, a good many in special education do not even recognize it. Behavior repression is not the solution for such deprived children.

While the school is a group work agency our own studies suggest that even in special classes there is little group work done. Since we know the group is often a more powerful agent than the adult, it is axiomatic that we must either select groups with the necessary qualities to provide what the mainstreamed special child needs or work through the group conditions which are counterindicated. This is seldom accomplished by consultation since group work itself is a very complicated process.

The research on how normal children in general respond to deviance has only begun—to say nothing of what might happen in any given classroom due to the idiosyncratic conditions. In a replication of earlier work by Kalter and Marsden, Hoffman (1976) has found that elementary age children can distinguish levels of pathology in described peers but their liking and disliking are independent of the level. Degree of disturbance does not always signify the degree of rejection. It is the disruptive or threatening character of the behavior which upsets the normal peer group. Regressive and immature behavior is often the most threatening. Gold (1958) has found four main dimensions in positive peer evaluation: expertness, physical attractiveness and prowess, social-emotional sensitivity, and skill and interests which are similar to peers. The very lack of these behaviors could be used to describe disturbed children. It is no wonder we have programs for these children which virtually "individualize out" any group involvement. The stark reality is that the peer culture can be a mainstream resource or disaster.

The Curricular Experience

To learn a fact or a skill can be therapeutic in itself. To see yourself as the slowest and lowest can be negative self-fulfillment. In an achievement-mad society—without special education protection—there are psychological messages all about. We have a right to ask, regarding mainstreaming, not only how much is the learning situation individualized but how much is the individualization accepted as a natural and inevitable condition. The careful scrutiny of many so-called open conditions indicates that to each his own is the way things are organized but if your "own" is to be low man on the totem pole, you have the curse. Providing psychological support for the child's state of accomplishment within the ethos of the typical classroom is the task.

There is a second part of the task factor in addition to the management of traditional curriculum elements. This is the affective educational enterprise. Since our special children are by definition having difficulty in the affective area, the utilization of affective education methodology becomes necessary. There are as many definitions of affective education as there are advocates, and as much confusion as direction in this field. Nonetheless, in mainstreaming a youngster, we need to attend to the breadth of the curriculum. In matter of fact, those few who appear to have the most impressive impact on the distraught child have moved so far from what a traditional classroom does that one has misgivings about finding the remedial environment in the typical regular or special education classroom. The bridge from the flexible special classroom to the typical regular classroom is a long one. The distance from the school-defined educational format to life-relevant programs for disturbed children may be too long to span. The few successful alternative schools may point the way. The degree to which these approaches have permeated the mainstream is also a question. One open elementary school (look—no inside walls at all!) absorbed all the problem kids who were able to just drift around in the low-pressure setting, but that is not special education accountability.

CONCLUSION

This book deals directly with the complications required to maximize the resources which can be generated in the mainstream. It is a truism that the very same generic elements constitute the conditions which create, acerbate, or restore. There are these adults, these peers, and these task experiences to consider. The psychological analysis of mainstreaming requires painstaking examination of what these elements produce relative to our best understanding of what is needed. It is necessary that we leave the fantasy world of decreeing arbitrary attributes and relevance to conditions whether they be the mainstream, the special class, or individual therapy. There should be many studies of "one special education boy's day" so that we begin to face up to the actual psychological transactions *vis-à-vis* the diagnostic prescription. Accountability is in the psychological substance of the experience. What must the socio-emotionally distraught child learn and where and how can it be provided? To speak of mainstreaming out of the psychological context can lead us astray.

REFERENCES

Cruickshank, W. M., and Johnson, G. O., eds. *Education of Exceptional Children and Youth.* Englewood Cliffs, N.J.: Prentice-Hall, 1975.

Finkel, N. J. *Mental Illness and Health: Its Legacy, Tensions, and Changes.* New York: Macmillan, 1976.

Gold, M. "Power in the Classroom." *Sociometry* 21 (1958): 50–60.

Henry, J. *Pathways to Madness.* New York: Random House, 1971.

Hoffman, E. "Children's Perceptions of their Emotionally Disturbed Peers." Unpublished Ph.D. dissertation, University of Michigan, 1976.

Kendall, D. "Towards Integration." *Special Education in Canada* (November 1971): 3–16.

King, C. "The Ego and the Integration of Violence in Homicidal Youth." *American Journal of Orthopsychiatry* 45 (1975): 134–45.

————. "Counter-Transference and Counter-Experience in the Treatment of Violence Prone Youth." *American Journal of Orthopsychiatry* 46 (1) (1976).

Love, L. R., and Kaswan, J. W. *Troubled Children: Their Families, Schools, and Treatments.* New York: Wiley-Interscience, 1974.

Morse, W. C. "Concepts Related to Diagnosis of Emotionally Impaired." In *State of the Art: Diagnosis and Treatment.* Monograph, Office of Education, U.S. Dept. of HEW, Bureau of Education for Handicapped, Cont. No. OEC-0-9-25290-4539(608), 1974.

————. "The Education of Socially Maladjusted and Emotionally Disturbed Children." In *Education of Exceptional Children and Youth,* edited by W. M. Cruickshank, 3rd. ed. New Jersey: Prentice-Hall, 1975.

————. *The Seriously Disturbed: Psycho-Social Disorders of Childhood and Youth.* Report to Hawaii Special Education Department, 1975.

————, and Cheney, C. "Psychodynamic Interventions in Emotional Disturbance." In *A Study of Child Variance,* edited by W. C. Rhodes. Vol. 2: *Interventions.* Conceptual Project in Emotional Disturbance. Ann Arbor, Michigan: University of Michigan, Institute for the Study of Mental Retardation and Related Disabilities, 1972.

————; Cutler, R. L.; and Fink, A. H. "Public School Classes for the Emotionally Handicapped: A Research Analysis." In *Conflict in the Classroom: The Education of Children with Problems,* edited by W. Morse, N. J. Long, and R. Newman. 2nd ed. Belmont, Calif.: Wadsworth, 1971.

Newman, R. G. *Groups in Schools. A Book about Teachers, Parents, and Children.* New York: Simon and Schuster, 1974.

Rhodes, W. C. "A Community Participation Analysis of Emotional Disturbance." *Exceptional Children* 36 (1970): 309–14.

3

Beyond Abnormality:
Into the Mainstream

WILLIAM C. RHODES

CHANGE

MAINSTREAMING IS A POSITIVE CATCHWORD expressing broad-scale hope in the possibility of institutional change. We seem to be borne upon a rising tide of goodwill toward our fellows and to be searching for ways out of the impass in the arena of human care. Mainstreaming cannot be considered independent of comparable social slogans currently in vogue. "Declassification," "deinstitutionalization," "child advocacy," and "due process" seem to be a small part of a single major impulse toward institutional change in this country.

My own inclination, after an intensive and extensive five-year survey of the arena of child variance which covered theory (Rhodes and Tracy 1972), intervention (Rhodes and Tracy 1973), and service delivery (Rhodes and Head 1974), leads me to predict that this impulse will alter our field quite considerably in the next ten years. In a fourth volume of speculation, based upon the Child Variance Studies (Rhodes 1975), I have tried to spell out some of the dynamic philosophical and value undercurrents beneath the concrete moves to mainstream declassify, and deinstitutionalize. Essentially, this volume points to a strongly developing countercurrent to all the established conventions in theory, practice, and service delivery in the child variance field, and it credits this countercurrent with considerable impact upon the field. Within this strong countercurrent can be distinguished the work of many individuals from quite diverse disciplines who criticized theory, practice, or systems.

In the area of theory, for instance, some of these individuals turned theory away from the target individuals who inspired it, toward the

31

society that created it, as Franz Fanon (1968) did in his analysis of white colonialism. Some rejected theory, as did Szasz (1970), who saw the model of psychopathology as a misrepresentation of human problems in living. Some carried the theory to its logical conclusion and startled us with the new implications, as did Marcuse (1955) in his rereading of Freud. Some raised questions about the political uses of theory where, as they saw it, theory was used to victimize and control individuals in the subordinate minorities or individuals who rebelled against the common convention. This was true of social deviance theorists such as Becker (1963) or Scheff (1966). Others analyzed the psychological uses of theory by the society, where unacceptable impulses were imputed to target individuals in the age-old process of scapegoating, i.e., Kvaraceus and Miller (1959) in relation to delinquency, Menninger (1968) in criminality, Foucault (1973) in relation to madness. Voices such as Goodman (1962), Laing (1964), Illich (1971), Holt (1964), Kozol (1967), and Brown (1973) are other representatives of countercurrent views.

The active dispensers of service who have legal responsibility for child problems are, like the teacher-conceptualizer, finding themselves in the center of a highly charged field of unrest and dissent. Activist convulsions are wracking the schools, correctional facilities, and welfare programs. Examples are the takeover and tyranny practiced by a group of adolescent girls in a mental health facility in New York City, the explosion at Attica, the racial confrontations in the Boston schools, the burning of school buses in Michigan, and the burning of offensive books in West Virginia. Such violent events in institutional systems dealing with human services are integrally linked to the conceptual unrest mentioned previously.

INTERPRETATIONS

The voices of strident protest and criticism and related institutional conclusions can be interpreted in several ways. One way is to question our own social sanity. We might say that the voices of doubt and aggression, the extreme acting out of both the client populations and the controlling hierarchy of the service institutions, are the social equivalent of individual madness. The madness will eventually have to be brought under control. The social acting out must be mastered by more reasonable forces so that life must go on as it was. Another way to view the raucous eruptions is to see this period as one of opening up of institutions, a stormy prelude to a new metamorphosis in which the institutions will continue to exist, but in considerably modified forms. The exact form is uncertain and indistinct at this point, but the remodeled institutions will be recognizable in their new guise, no matter how altered. Finally, one may view the current rumblings and agitation as a beginning of the end of centralized, monolithic human-service institutions. Schools as we know them will disappear. Prisons are on their way out. Mental institutions, as distinct islands of separation from the general society, will recede into history.

Actually, any of the alternative outcomes are possible. My own reading of the countercurrent literature concludes that the first alternative is extremely unlikely unless this nation repudiates its history and veers very strongly in the authoritarian and totalitarian direction, because the disaffection is so widespread. Signs of unrest and self-criticism expressed in modification words such as mainstreaming and in the analysis of the antithesis voices such as Szasz, Illich, and Marcuse, add up to a new social consciousness with regard to human variance. Our world view seems to be changing, or rather, the outline of a new world view is beginning to emerge in brief segments of the society. The institutions as we have known them are a product of another world view, another social state of consciousness. Unless this new world view is attacked by force, it is likely to have an impact upon the minds of the general public and the old world view will be either undermined or strongly diluted.

As a result of our studies in child variance and an analysis of the vast primary and secondary sources we have researched and reviewed, one of the other two alternatives are likely to occur. Either human-service institutions, like schools, will undergo considerable metamorphosis, or they will totally crumble and other forms of the human-service function will reappear in our society. My own hopes for the future, based upon the strong new surge of tolerance and humanism in the antithesis views of human and child variance and the influence it seems to exert upon such mini-movements as mainstreaming, lean very heavily toward the latter alternative—that is, a gradual dissolution of the centralized monolithic, hierarchic, bureaucratic form of human-care institutions, including schools.

AFTER ABNORMALITY

Directly connected to these general trends, we seem also to be undergoing specific focused changes in the social consciousness of differences or deviance in children and their adult counterparts. Our child variance studies indicate a breakdown in the general and specific categories by which we were able to divide children into normal and abnormal groups. Our established theories began with a premise of normal and abnormal; then we set up explanatory systems which would account for such differences at the same time that they provided a basis for the sorting of children. The proliferation of theoretical conceptions of deviance or differences seems to be an index of the difficulty we had in making such clear sortings. Psychodynamic theories, behavioral theories, sociological theories, biogenic theories, and ecological theories are indices of these sorting and explanatory difficulties. In spite of great efforts represented in these theoretical models, we moved no closer toward agreement with regard to what deviance is, and who is deviant, in 1975 than in 1875. In any area of differences, mental retardation, emotional disturbance, delinquency, learning disabilities, we are completely unable to reach consensus with regard to what we are talking about. Our elaborate theories do not help us. Therefore, we are beginning to suspect that there is something very artificial and meaningless in normality-abnormality distinctions which underlie many of these theories. Normality-abnormality in most areas of problems in people is a cultural mind-trap and little else. It may even have elements of a genetic mind-trap. It gives us a sense of security and sureness with respect to who "we" are and who "they" are. It provides a sense of clan solidarity long after the closeness and security of clan have receded dimly in our social history. It provides a sense of identity and belonging, a psychological union which we seem to need so desperately. But as a measure of certainty it has eluded us altogether. We have traveled the route of science to try to pin down with precision such differentiated abnormality terms as schizophrenia, delinquency, mental retardation, minimal brain damage, and emotional disturbance, but it has been a frustrating and elusive search in each instance. We are no closer, and our differential theories, as they try to close in on normality-abnormality, are no nearer to us than they were when we first began developing our scientific instruments which were intended to bring these human conditions under the microscope and reveal them once and for all.

Even worse than being a cultural mind-trap for us, as soon as the linguistic trigger of normality-abnormality is tripped, our minds, our personalities, our responses shut down, close tight, and rigidify around this anachronistic trigger from our clan past. All of the feelings and behaviors associated with that atavistic trigger are fully aroused and begin functioning to protect us from the threat coming in from outside. We restrict our attention, develop tunnel vision, and ignore the wide range of cues, behaviors, signals, and sending waves coming in from the person caught in the narrow sights of our internal trigger. It is like a haze that closes around that sender out there to color everything he or she says or does with the clan alarm of strangeness that is triggered in us. Everything about the sender is a threat to us and our identity as a clan member. Our actions as individuals and as a collective are aimed at defusing or normalizing the threat and preserving our own identity and safety. Whether we treat him, or imprison him, proselytize him or teach him, we are trying to normalize him so that our sense of safety, security, and identity can be restored. Once this sense is restored we can begin functioning more fully; our range of senses can open up to the full environment; and the flexibility and richness of our total behavioral repertoire can begin functioning again.

This is how I view normalizing and, to a certain extent, mainstreaming. This is not meant in a carping or criticizing sense. My own assessment of efforts such as mainstreaming, normalizing, deinstitutionalizing, litigation, and decategorizing, adds up to optimism and hope. I believe we are trying very hard to move beyond the cultural mind-trap of normal-abnormal, particularly with regard to children. However, our movement is intuitive and dream-like. It is a form of sleep-walking. It is as though we know deep inside ourselves what we are moving toward and away from, without a preestablished rational base. This, too, is a hopeful sign. It is much deeper and more psychologically meaningful than many of our cognitive, pragmatic social actions. A deep, new consciousness is stirring within the shared psyche of our society, a new clan sense of the outsider, a new psycho-social incorporation taking the place of the repellent response inherited from our ancestral consciousness.

It is a very uneven process. Like all dream-action, it is kaleidoscopic, jumbled, fuzzy, irrational, full of conflicting information and behavior. I believe that the logical next step is for society to gain full insight into what is rumbling underneath and consciously put aside the psychological and social mind-structure of normal-abnormal. We need to move beyond the fear of deviation and diversity, toward a conscious acceptance of diversity and a celebration of deviance. It would open the way for liberation of both the deviant and the deviant-watcher from oppressive bonds and offer the mainstream as their natural habitat.

A SOCIAL TIME BOMB

Mainstreaming now has a limited referent for a special group of child-care people. Its limited referent is the school and its relevance is for the educator and the educational process. However, ticking inside that simple word is a social time bomb. It signifies the possibility of overt, external realization in everyday life of all manners of divergences and differences in people. It means granting an equal status to forms of being which have been subjugated, restricted, controlled, and allowed limited and circumscribed existence. Gays speak about "coming out." Essentially this means exposing to light certain characteristics and ways of being that are carefully isolated and hidden from overt existence in everyday life. On the personal side, it means acceptance of and proclaiming oneself, demanding equality, and openly living as one is. It means refusing to defer to public subterfuge, the denial of certain human traits and characteristics. Mainstreaming is the social counterpart of such operational inclusion, previously denied, of human traits and characteristics in public policy and public practice. It is a new social attitude, a liberalization of the culture, and a broadening of the base of social inclusion.

In our now limited use of the word, *mainstreaming* means inclusion of labeled children in the main educational stream. It means attempting to grant equality of citizenship within the school. However, now that mandatory education is becoming a reality, it will, more and more, mean inclusion of previously abnormalized children in the mainstream of life outside the school. All of the professional processes of abnormalization —including the clinical enterprise, the professional role, service-delivery chauvinism—will have to be reexamined and questioned as we move further into the mainstream. We are drifting onto the stage of this profound social drama like sleepwalking actors, but the curtain is about to go up and the audience out there is waiting for the action to begin.

In the next stage of this drama the audience will have to be included more and more. The separation between professional and public will have to begin to blur. The normalization process cannot be accomplished simply within the service-delivery channels and the professional community. These channels and the special community are not the mainstream. Furthermore, as previously discussed in this chapter, the normality-abnormality distinctions have been heavily dependent on a collective consensus with respect to which human traits and states are to be included and excluded in the mainstream. The process can be changed only when the consensus begins to weaken. The thesis of this chapter has been that the consensus is breaking down, the categories are beginning to dissolve in the public mind. In the rising tide of goodwill and broadening tolerance, firm lines between normal and abnormal, between mainstream and non-mainstream are being breached.

The professional body has to realize this and move to consolidate the social gains which have been made. *Mainstream* has to be reinterpreted. The American mainstream is democratization and diversity. The movement toward declassifying and normalization is an American mainstream movement. The legend on the Statue of Liberty states our explicit intention as a nation to be a polyglot nation, open as a haven to populations considered deviant and unwanted in other nations. Embracing diversity and deviation has been our strength. Mainstreaming in this larger sense means that our institutions and processes have to accommodate diversity, have to be formulated and constructed so that the widest possible range of differences can be accorded full respect and social viability. In returning to our roots, we have to provide for cultural pluralism, institutional pluralism, and pluralism in traits and life styles.

If we translate this into the role of education, the special educator's function in mainstreaming now becomes twofold: (1) education of the general public and the educational community with respect to normalization—that is, including child diversity and deviation in the social and institutional mainstream; and (2) changing the educational structures and processes to embrace diversity and pluralism.

Before undertaking these two tasks, special education and human-service personnel who feel committed to such policies would have to undergo shifts in their own perspectives and a reordering of their own knowledge base. The heavy drag of abnormality imagery is lodged deep in our minds. The reversion to such attitudes and orientations are a constant source of discouragement even to the most avant-gard thinkers among us. It is like an atavistic engram in the brain which may retreat in the background for long periods of quiescence and then suddenly flare up again. Our own earlier concepts betray us, and our perseveration thinking returns us again and again to classification and segregation. It is the kind of process, for instance, which we see going on right now in psychiatry and psychology in relationship to homosexuality. Both official bodies have de-pathologized the behavior and concluded that it is merely variance in sex and yet their therapists continue to "treat" the condition. We find the same thing happening to sociologists interested in social deviance who study and work with educational and service agencies. They become enmeshed in the pathology categories of their clinical counterparts and try to incorporate the clinical model into their work.

The special educator who moves toward mainstreaming, normalization, and systems definitions seems to have to undergo a reconversion experience in which his initial commitment toward human service and human care is resurfaced and strengthened. This is not simply a cognitive restructuring process; it is also a deep affective experience. It requires value search, consciousness raising, and personal encounter with oneself. It requires a personal decathexis of the "abnormalizing" structures of child-care systems, at least a temporary removal of the external contingencies, such as diagnosis and treatment which counteract the behaviors associated with normalizing and mainstreaming. This move beyond abnormality also requires a supportive community or support system of fellow believers. Eventually, it will require external ego-supports and rewards which are more heavily directed toward normalizing than toward abnormalizing. Finally, it seems almost a necessity to undergo an identity crisis, in which one's own connection to the excluded and abnormalized population becomes an issue. We must undergo a breakdown of our own fears of becoming "one of them," our horror at moving to the other side to which they are relegated by the controlling forces of society. Such an experience is like a conversion. It is a turning loose of one's long socialization into a stylized reality and awakening into another view of the world and one's place in that world. Everything is transformed. It is almost a transcending process whereby suddenly one is on the other side, has become one with the rejected populations, and feels quite warm and comfortable in the new identification. This transformation is much more than an intellectual integration of the political, psychological, and ecological bases of abnormalization. In recent years our research and our theory have brought new understandings of the social and psychic processes working in our individual and social dynamics which causes us to sweep some of our members onto the other side of the wall. The scientific evidence for a collective repetition-compulsion for ritual sacrifice of our fellow members has eroded theoretical models of social and psychic pathology upon scientist-professionals. Now it is scientifically defensible to attack psychopathology models. However, the deviance realization discussed here is much more than a cognitive comprehension of the state of our abnormalized population. It is a peak experience of identification and celebration, where the tables are completely turned and one embraces the extruded and unacceptable part of oneself and others. The ambiance surrounding deviance changes completely. The reality flooding our minds is no longer the brooding grey of diagnosis and treatment, but the brilliant colors of celebration. It is a new consciousness of the human state arrived at with the whole being, rather than just the intellect.

It is probably that only a few people actually achieve this full sense of change. The socialization into pathology and the consequent saturation of pathology imagery in our social and individual consciousness, the external supports for pathologizing behavior existing in our professional organizations, service systems, theories, and intervention technologies is such a powerful set of resistants for us that peak realization may be very difficult. However, deliberate, conscious exploration of oneself and of the antithetical reality inherent in deviance celebration is a necessary first step toward reeducation of the community and remodeling caregiving structures toward embracing diversity and pluralism. A personal immersion process seems to be almost a necessary prelude to action-taking.

Reeducation of the general populace will be a slow process, but the effort could join forces with the other humanistic reeducation efforts in progress across the nation. The liberation of attitudes about minorities and about women should provide precedent and models by which to proceed. While scientific arguments can be included to forward the case that the major portion of the labeled populations are social hostages, the main appeal to attitude change will probably best be made on the same grounds as women's liberation or minority liberation. It is a matter of conscience and justice. The humanitarian argument will have to be the base. An appeal to the deep, positive, caring impulses in this nation is the most direct educational route. Our nation was founded upon an ideology of care and haven. It is a powerful strain in our collective psyche. There is a strong sentiment for justice and equality in our makeup. We are a nation formed, originally, as a source of compassion for the oppressed across the world.

In terms of institutional and structural change, the present conditions provide fertile ground for efforts along these lines. The organizational structures of educational and service agencies are in considerable disarray at this time. They are straining under the pressures of conflicting interests which are bound together in the total system. The consumer constituency is contesting the reality governing the service actions of the administering bureaus. The consumer constituency challenges the bureau services (for instance, the growing revolt of prison populations against the criminal ethic and its substitution of a political prisoner ideology; the litigant challenges of minorities to classification and categorical programming in schools). The service staffs are unionizing to present their case and to protect their interests. The administering bureaus are hardening their guidelines and increasing their monitoring and accountability forces.

The service structures are also reeling from the multiple assaults of larger social issues which are being played out upon the stage of their operational patterns. Schools are the battleground of minority issues— whether these are racial or ideological. There is black against white,

Spanish-American against Anglo, etc., at the same time that we are seeing the ultra free-school constituency battling the ultra-structured school constituency in places like Prince Georges County, Maryland, or West Virginia. The feminist and various "rights" movements are adding to the organizational, structural, and program strains of these service institutions.

Under these multiple strains and forces, the agencies and systems of federal, state, and local education and service are becoming chaotic. The divisive forces and philosophies within the massive, hierarchical, and vertically determined structures of education and human services is beginning to have a specific effect upon the governmentally funded and controlled systems. The previous coalition of political, professional, and public forces is breaking up. The concept of a unified solution to human needs being administered through a centralized bureau operating upon a single, consensual philosophy of education and service is beginning to give way to a new view of serving social well-being. This view takes into account the diversity of peoples, cultures, needs, and values in our democratic society. It argues for pluralism and diverse group identities as the determining foundation for human caregiving functions of the nation. It argues against a massive unified structure as the administering agent for education and caregiving. It argues against lodging caring in centralized service bureaus and organized professional forces.

It says to the committed individuals who have given their lives to service, "You have to make the transition to a new identification. The old one is no longer viable. You have to take on a new role—celebrant of the segregated populations to whom you have made your life commitment." This leads to action centering around transformation of the systems themselves into instruments of self-realization for pluralistic segments of the population, with diverse aims and diverse organizational structures. It means transformation of the focus of these caregiving systems from normalizing a small non-normal population, to self-relegation of widely diverse self-identified groups. It means inclusion of diversity in a much broadened mainstream of social life.

SUMMARY

These observations are conclusions which seem to emerge out of current trends in caregiving philosophy and action as viewed against the background of our *Studies in Child Variance*. To repeat them in a condensed summary statement, it seems that the concept of mainstreaming has much broader implications than we have fully realized. Furthermore, it is not an isolated programmatic phenomenon, but part of a larger, more inclusive process occurring in the field of child variance and the society in general. We are struggling with our entanglement in the meanings of normal-abnormal, and in the dim recesses of our individual and collective minds, we are trying to move beyond abnormality. Some of us who have been most deeply involved in that struggle have come to a new state of mind which celebrates diversity and deviance and which identifies the so-called consumers of service as our own reference group. These groups are part of ourselves struggling for recognition and acceptance in our imperfect, human state, asking for inclusion in the social mainstream of such a human condition.

The new state of mind views caregiving in a different light. It adds new form to the change efforts being attempted in mainstreaming, declassification, deinstitutionalization, and due-process. It suggests strong decentralization, democratization, and pluralization of the service structures. It asks that education and human care become the instruments of diverse, self-identified groups, which set their own course, their own organizational forms, and their own monitoring systems.

Within the ecological perspective, such a move to diversification in education and caregiving provides a wide range of environments into which diverse personalities and life styles can find a fit. Normalizing, mainstreaming, deinstitutionalizing would be opening social channels to multiple and pluralistic environments rather than single, uniform agencies of caring. For those of us who have gone through a profound change in perspective, this would be the social concretizing of the celebration of deviance.

REFERENCES

Becker, H. *Outsiders: Studies in the Sociology of Deviance.* New York: Free Press, 1963.

Brown, P. "Social Change at Harrowdale State Hospital: Impression II." In *Rough Times,* edited by J. Agel. New York: Ballantine, 1973.

Fanon, F. *The Wretched of the Earth.* New York: Grove, 1968.

Foucault, M. *Madness and Civilization.* New York: Random House, 1973.

Goodman, P. *Compulsory Mis-education and the Community of Scholars.* New York: Vintage, 1962.

Holt, J. *How Children Fail.* New York: Pittman, 1964.

Illich, I. *Deschooling Society.* New York: Harper & Row, 1971.

Kozol, J. *Death at an Early Age.* Boston: Houghton Mifflin, 1967.

Kvaraceus, W., and Miller, W. *Delinquent Behavior: Culture and Individual.* Washington, D.C.: National Educational Association, 1959.

Laing, R. *The Divided Self.* London: Tavistock, 1964.

Marcuse, H. *Eros and Civilization.* New York: Random House, 1955.

Menninger, K. "The Crime of Punishment." *Saturday Review* (September 7, 1968).

Rhodes, W. C. *A Study of Child Variance. Volume IV: The Future.* Ann Arbor: University of Michigan Press, 1975.

————, and Head, S. *A Study of Child Variance. Volume III: Service Delivery Systems.* Ann Arbor: University of Michigan Press, 1974.

————, and Tracy, M. *A Study of Child Variance. Volume I: Conceptual Models.* Ann Arbor: University of Michigan Press, 1972.

————, and Tracy, M. *A Study of Child Variance. Volume II: Interventions.* Ann Arbor: University of Michigan Press, 1973.

Scheff, T. *Being Mentally Ill.* Chicago: Aldine, 1966.

Szasz, T. *Ideology and Insanity.* New York: Doubleday, 1970.

4

Legal Implications

H. RUTHERFORD TURNBULL III

THE PARAMETERS OF THE PROBLEM

A DISCUSSION OF THE LEGAL IMPLICATIONS of mainstreaming emotionally disturbed children confronts two problems. First, there is almost no law directly on point. None of the reported cases dealing with the suspension or expulsion of a pupil from school on the ground that the pupil is emotionally disturbed or disturbing make findings of fact about the pupil's emotional capacities or disabilities, the effect of the school on the child's emotional capacities or disabilities, or the relationship between the child's emotional state and actions and the school's action of suspending or expelling the child for behavior that may be related to the child's emotional state. Second, with few exceptions, the law of special education has been developed principally in litigation involving the mentally retarded.

We are guided largely by the general principle that, once procedural due process requirements are satisfied, a pupil's education can be terminated for either a short term through suspension or a longer period through expulsion; the widely recognized importance of education to the pupil and to society is no barrier (McClung 1974). The present limitations on the school's power to suspend or expel a pupil, after a due process hearing, are, in the main, judicially imposed but they are not yet significant safeguards of the pupil's right to education. They consist primarily of the requirements that school authorities not act maliciously, in bad faith, arbitrarily, or unreasonably; in short, they consist of the application of principles of equal protection, substantive due process (the principle that a person may not be arbitrarily deprived of property, or, as the courts have interpreted "property," an educational opportunity) and *ultra vires* (the principle that the school authorities may not exceed the powers granted to them by regulations, statutes, or constitution). Arbitrariness may consist of applying one code of school rules and its sanctions in an uneven manner, as, for example, by applying the code to blacks or males but not applying it in the same manner to whites or females. Unreasonableness may occur when the sanction overreaches the offense, as where a pupil is expelled for a relatively minor infraction of school rules. Malicious or bad faith action might consist of a schoolman's exercising suspension or expulsion powers not granted to him. Principles of equal protection, substantive due process and *ultra vires* may be brought to bear in these cases. But proving unreasonable action has been difficult. Rarely has an opportunity been granted to the pupil before the suspension or expulsion occurs to prove the schoolman was acting unreasonably, and even when a prior due process hearing was available, the presumption of correct actions favored the schoolman and the burden rested on the student.

Moreover, the state does itself and the affected pupil no good by terminating the pupils education, even after a due process hearing. Indeed, it may substantially harm the pupil (by stigmatizing him) if the reasons for its actions were based on the ground that the pupil is emotionally disturbed.

The Supreme Court's recent decision in *Goss v. Lopez* (419 U.S. 565, 1975) will have a significant impact on school suspension practices. In *Goss,* the court held that due process requires, in connection with a suspension of a pupil for up to ten days, that the pupil be given oral or written notice of the charges against him and, if he denies them, an explanation of the evidence the authorities have and an opportunity to present his or her version of the facts. *Goss* establishes, without doubt, the right of a pupil to a prior due process hearing in all circumstances except those where his presence in school endangers persons or property there or threatens the disruption of the academic process, thus justifying his immediate removal from school. Among other things, it will affect most school suspensions of a significant duration; the Court found that a ten-day suspension is *de minimis*. Where the Court will find that a *de minimis* point is reached is not clear, but the usual two- or three-day suspensions now seem safe from due process requirements. It also will generally provide the student with an opportunity to raise defenses of malicious, bad faith, arbitrary or unreasonable action before the schoolman can act. It may redress the power relationship between the student and the schoolman. And it may make the termination of the benefits of education, which the Court recognized to be subsumed under the "property" and "liberty" guarantees of the due process clause, all the more difficult for the schoolman, with the result that the school and society will not be as quick to spite itself by denying the benefits of education to a student and to injure the student by suspending him.

It is with these considerations in mind that an inquiry now must be made from the lawyer's peculiar point of view into the whys and wherefores of mainstreaming.

MAINSTREAMING: WHAT IS IT, AND WHY?

So far as the law is concerned, mainstreaming reflects a judicial and legislative preference that, whenever a student is to be placed or tracked, he shall be included in a regular, "normal" track in preference to a special education track and that he shall be educated in the regular school environment rather than in the confines of a special school. Mainstreaming is no more than a *preference* in favor of regular educational placement. Because mainstreaming reflects a preference, it is not, nor should it become, an inflexible rule; rather, it should be a guide for conduct, not a rule of conduct. As a guide, it should not prohibit alternatives to mainstream placement.

Why is mainstreaming a judicial and legislative preference? The reasons are many. The preference is a reaction to the exclusion of children with special needs from both the opportunity for education (placement in a school system) and the opportunity for a meaningful education (placement in an appropriate program).

It is a reaction to the view historically accepted by many educators and institutionalized in school practices that children with special needs are different from, and therefore should be excluded from, education with "normal" children. It attempts to protect exceptional children from the stereotype that they are all different and deficient. It is a method for individualizing an exceptional pupil's education, since mainstreaming, as applied, prevents a child's being placed in special programs except if it is first determined that the child cannot profit from regular educational placement.

Mainstreaming is preferred because the existence of separate, self-contained special education programs and schools was found to be equivalent to the establishment of separate but unequal systems of education. Separate has generally meant unequal, and special education has not been equated with equal educational opportunities. Some courts have found, as a matter of fact, and some commentators have demonstrated that the pattern and practice of some schools had been to assign the "worst" children, typically those with special needs, to the least capable teachers, to put them in the most inferior facilities, to provide them with less than adequate educational materials, and to fund special education programs less generously than normal "mainstream" programs. Seen in this light, mainstreaming shares some of the strategies of racial integration of the schools.

One strategy behind racial integration was to integrate a racial minority into the racial mainstream. The hope behind the strategy was that the racial majority would not neglect its children's education in integrated schools and that the continued attention of the white majority to "quality education" would assure that the black minority would be given the same type of education as the white majority. The same strategy and the same hopes underlie the preference for mainstreaming exceptional children. It is undoubtedly true that special education, among other systems imperfectly serving or indeed discriminating against the handicapped, is the new civil rights battlefield.

Mainstreaming is a reaction to the terminal aspects of special education. The placement of exceptional children in self-contained special education programs has never been the first, but always the last, step in the child's educational development. It was the final placement. The preference for mainstreaming rests on the hope that the self-fulfilling prophecies and the self-limiting characteristics of special educational placement will not be the end result for children with special needs.

Finally, mainstreaming is preferred because it is widely and forcefully advocated by many educators and consumers. If mainstreaming is not desirable, it is incumbent on educators to offer the courts and legislatures acceptable alternatives. This is an important but not well-recognized point. The courts and legislatures are not equipped to prescribe what the education of emotionally disturbed or other handicapped students should consist of. They are essentially equipped only to respond to the imprecations of educators, the advocacy of litigants, the exigencies of the public's attitude, and the government's fiscal capacities. In attempting to "do right" for the emotionally disturbed child, they are now required to choose among a limited number of alternative approaches. They may choose to set a policy of mainstreaming, to attempt to improve the special education system with or without imposing on it any preferences for mainstreaming, to do both, or to do neither. In considering the claims of the handicapped pupil, the courts have chosen the routes of declaring a policy preference for the mainstream and ordering improvements in the special education system itself. They have set a direction into the mainstream while at the same time recognizing the value of separate, self-contained special education. Legislatures have tended to follow suit.

But if Rhodes (Chapter 3) is correct in suggesting that our concepts of education are atomizing, if it is true as Paul (Chapter 1) suggests that there is no agreement among educators about what to do for the emotionally disturbed child, much less how to do it, and if it is true that, in response to the atomization of our beliefs about the purposes and nature of education for the emotionally disturbed, many educators latch onto a concept—mainstreaming—and pursue it singlemindedly and blindly, then the lawmaker is faced with a cruel problem. He is asked (by litigants if he is a judge or by agencies and constituents if he is a legislator) to choose among a limited number of responses, as suggested above, or to create the possibility of an increased number of responses. In the absence of consensus among educators, litigants, and constituents, the lawmaker's decision to choose among a limited number of responses, such as mainstreaming, improving special education as a separate system of education, or doing both or neither, may limit the educational opportunities for the pupils he most seeks to serve. But if he seeks to create additional educational alternatives and a wider range of choices (for example, mainstreaming, improving special education as a separate system, doing both or neither, or providing a disunified system of educational alternatives, one that permits the emotionally disturbed child an opportunity to receive the necessary academic training without necessarily participating in the traditional academic or school environment), then he is limited: (1) if he is a judge, by the educational system to which his orders run, the courts' inherent caution in carving out new social policy, and the need for his orders to be acceptable if he also wants them to be obeyed; and (2) if he is a legislator, by the many factors affecting legislative policy-making, including, among others, fiscal considerations, constituent reaction, agency resistance, and the preferences of his legislative colleagues. Thus, if mainstreaming should not be the preferred policy for the courts and legislatures to adopt, it is not only difficult for the lawmaker to say which policy is to be preferred, but it also is incumbent on educators to provide the lawmaker with acceptable alternatives.

THE ELUSIVE STANDARDS

Lawyers look for precise terms to insure that substantive due process obtains in each case. The due process issue is a simple one of definitions.

What do the terms "emotionally disturbed" and "socially maladjusted" mean? When a child is suspended or excluded from school because he is emotionally disturbed or socially maladjusted, or when he is taken from the mainstream and placed in a special education track because he is emotionally disturbed or socially maladjusted, he is subjected to state action on the basis of terms that may well be unconstitutionally vague. He is made subject to state action on the basis of terms that connote social values, are culturally derived, and are value-laden. The problem is that state action based on such loosely defined terms has a great potential for being so abusive and arbitrary that substantive due process considerations are immediately raised. Moreover, the potential for abuse —the risk of arbitrary school action that does not conform to principles of substantive due process—is especially damaging not simply because it exists, but because the action connotes something deficient about the pupil. It tends to make him suffer not only from potentially arbitrary action but also from the stigma of being different and deficient.

The major problem of applying legal principles to the placement, suspension, or exclusion of the emotionally disturbed child is that the basis for the action is often so elusive that principles of substantive due process may not reach the action. It is one thing to apply substantive due process to the educational placement of the mentally retarded person; it is quite another to apply it to the emotionally disturbed.

The basis for classifying the mentally retarded pupil usually is the child's performance on IQ or other standardized tests. These tests are subject to criticism on the grounds that they are culturally and socio-economically biased, improperly administered, or administered to persons for whom the tests clearly are inappropriate. If in any given instance a test is thus inappropriate for the student, the educator's reliance on the test results as a basis for classifying the student and placing him in a special educational program is subject to the attack on the substantive due process grounds that the action is unreasonable and arbitrary.

It is difficult to apply the same theory to the classification of a pupil as emotionally disturbed. There are undoubtedly students who clearly and indisputably are emotionally disturbed—their behavior is such that few competent psychiatrists or psychologists would disagree that they are emotionally disturbed. Moreover, the psychiatrists or psychologists would tend to agree that the standards for their judgment are sound— the standards are not culturally or socio-economically biased, their tests are properly administered, and they are administered to persons for whom they are appropriate. In these relatively few instances, the classification (labeling the students emotionally disturbed and placing them in special educational programs for the emotionally disturbed) cannot be attacked on substantive due process grounds as being unreasonable and therefore arbitrary.

But there are many persons who are not clearly and indisputably emotionally disturbed. They are nevertheless liable to being classified as emotionally disturbed. Several basic and initial questions exist with respect to these "borderline" persons. Do medical criteria of emotional disturbance apply to them? Behavioral criteria? Do both or neither apply? How does the applicable statute define, if it indeed does define, "emotionally disturbed" or "socially maladjusted"? In the great majority of instances of "borderline" students, the standards for determining whether the pupil is emotionally disturbed or socially maladjusted are not clear. There is, moreover, no widespread agreement among the professionals about the meaning of "emotionally disturbed" or "socially maladjusted" in those cases. Accordingly, there is no standard by which the courts may be guided in judging whether the educator's action (classification) is reasonable and thus above reproach on substantive due process grounds, or arbitrary and thus vulnerable to substantive due process attack.

The problem of standards is further complicated by the fact that the educator frequently applies the standards of "normal" or "acceptable" behavior in deciding whether a child's behavior evidences emotional disturbance or social maladjustment. The meaning of "normal" or "acceptable" is so disputable, so value-laden, and so culturally and socio-economically biased that the difficulties of applying standards and thus of determining whether substantive due process applies are exacerbated and may not be justiciable. If a matter is not justiciable, the potential for arbitrariness by the educator is unchecked and thus unlimited.

If, on the other hand, the standard is dangerous to one's self or others or disruptive of the school environment, the standards are not nearly so elusive and thus are far more justiciable. Typically, however, the reported decisions involving classification, suspension, or expulsion of pupils who are either dangerous or disruptive inquire only into the child's behavior, not into its causes. Courts look to the student's action and thus merely to the symptoms of his problems. They do not inquire into the causes for his action or what underlies the symptoms.

Despite the serious shortcomings of the principles of substantive due process with respect to the emotionally disturbed student, there are no similar shortcomings with respect to the principles of procedural due process and equal protection. The Supreme Court's *Goss* decision does not spell out in detail the nature of the procedural due process hearing required to be granted to any pupil who is suspended or expelled, but it does make it clear that some form of due process hearing is required—either immediately before the suspension or expulsion or very shortly thereafter. Moreover, the equal protection guarantee requires that like cases be treated alike, so that the educator's action in the case of one emotionally disturbed student, however arbitrary it may be and however unsusceptible to substantive due process attack, is constitutionally required to be replicated in identical or similar cases.

THE INTEREST ANALYSIS

Some persons have argued (Weintraub and Abeson 1972) that the recent cases establishing the right to education of mentally handicapped students have the effect of guaranteeing a new type of access to education (no longer is equal access to a school system the minimum that may be required of educators by exceptional children; the minimum now extends to equal access to different resources for different purposes). Others have argued that the cases have the effect of providing individualized education (Kirp et al. 1974) (this requirement derives from the mandate that procedural due process hearings be granted before a pupil is placed outside of the mainstream; it also derives from the mandate that the pupil's education be "appropriate" or "suited" to him). If these commentators are correct, then the cases and their effects have significant implications with respect to whether and, if so, under what circumstances an emotionally disturbed student should be mainstreamed.

If the educator is indeed required to furnish equal access to different resources for different purposes and to individualize the pupil's education to the maximum extent practicable, it will be helpful to him in determining the extent of his obligations to rely on the lawyer's customary "interest analysis." This is a method of inquiry into the legal relationships of the educator, the pupil, and other affected persons. It asks who has what interest with respect to whom—it raises issues about whose interests are at stake, what the interests are, and under what circumstances do some interests prevail over other potentially conflicting or competing interests.

An interest analysis first focuses on what is at stake, the issue. Is it the pupil's failure to behave in "normal" or "acceptable" ways? Is his behavior disruptive? Or, is his behavior dangerous to himself and others?

Unless and until a prior determination is made about what is at stake and what the issue is, as evidenced by the student's behavior, it will be difficult to pinpoint whether the student's interests are the same as or different from his parents, and whether their joint or separate interests are the same as or different from the educator's. In short, unless it is made clear at the outset that the issue is one of three types of behavior, then it is unlikely that it will become clear who has what interests, whose interests are affected by the action that may be taken, how those interests are affected, who has concomitant rights and duties with respect to others, and whose interests should outweigh another's.

If we can identify the various rights and duties, then the respective weight of various interests and the procedures for balancing and asserting them may present themselves more clearly. For example, such simplified rights and duties may be: (1) in the case of the lack of "normal" or "acceptable" behavior—on the pupil's part, the duty to conform generally to the social mores of the school environment; on the parent's part, the duty to reinforce conformity without stifling the pupil's individuality; and on the school's part, the duty to continue the process of education and develop a greater tolerance and acceptance of nonconforming behavior; (2) in the case of disruptive behavior—on the pupil's part, the duty to desist from disruptive behavior; on the parent's part, the duty to engage in family counselling for the parent; (3) in the case of behavior that is "dangerous to one's self or others"—on the pupil's part, the duty to desist; on the parent's part, the duty to obtain counseling for the pupil; and on the school's part, the duty to protect other students and its staff, to continue the child's educational process (self-contained and separate education) and to provide counseling services.

To help determine the interests at stake, it is useful to determine who wants what from whom and why? The parents may want their child to be mainstreamed, and indeed they may benefit by their child being mainstreamed. They may seek to avoid the social opprobrium of having their child classified as an emotionally disturbed child, and they may indeed avoid that stigma if their child is mainstreamed. Moreover, they may want their child mainstreamed to prevent him from being stigmatized and because mainstream education may be educationally appropriate.

The child's interests, on the other hand, may conflict with the parents'. He may want to avoid the mainstream and may indeed benefit from special educational placement if mainstreaming would not provide him with an appropriate or suitable education. He may also seek to avoid the mainstream because, once in it, he runs a greater risk of being excluded from it by suspension or expulsion than if he is in the sometimes more hospitable and more tolerating environment of special education. He may likewise resist mainstreaming because, once in the mainstream, he may become functionally excluded from education by not being able to take advantage of the education offered because it is inappropriate to his capacities or disabilities. He may seek to avoid the mainstream because it denies him the access to which he is entitled—equal access to different resources. Finally, he may object to being mainstreamed because he may well be labeled as emotionally disturbed without being furnished the more appropriate education that a special track might provide. That is, if he will be known as emotionally disturbed in the mainstream, he is not relieved of the stigma and he runs the risk of losing the potentially beneficial aspects of special education placement. On the other hand, he may be better served by mainstreaming than by special education if he thereby is relieved of the risk of stigma and simultaneously provided an appropriate education.

And what of the educator? His interests, likewise, are many and varied. On the one hand, he may object to mainstreaming the emotionally disturbed child because the child is potentially dangerous to himself and others (students and faculty) and/or because the child might disrupt the education of others. He may also object because the faculty in the normal track may not have the ability or the willingness to cope with and train the emotionally disturbed child or because the faculty in the special track are clearly more qualified and willing to do so. On the other hand, he may seek to mainstream the child because it will provide the child with better educational opportunities, because it satisfies judicial or legislative preferences for the mainstream, because it avoids stigmatizing the child, or because it may obviate the procedural due process hearing that might attend placement in the special education track.

PRESUMPTIONS, PROCEDURAL SAFEGUARDS, AND INQUIRIES

It is relevant to have identified some of the interests that may be at stake. To have done so may have helped to delineate and balance them (and thus advance the resolution of their conflict). Given the judicial and legislative preferences for mainstreaming, it also may suggest that certain legal presumptions should be indulged and certain rules on the elements and burdens of proof and related procedural safeguards should be forthcoming.

If the issue—if what is at stake—is the child's failure to engage in "normal" or "acceptable" behavior, the presumption in favor of mainstreaming and against special education placement and the sanctions of suspension or exclusion should be stronger than if the issue is "disruption" or "danger to one's self or others." If the issue is "disruption," the presumption in favor of mainstreaming should be stronger than if it is "danger to one's self or others" and weaker than if it is the lack of "normal" or "acceptable" behavior. If the issue is "danger to one's self or others," the presumption against mainstreaming and in favor of special educational placement and the sanctions of suspension or expulsion should be stronger than if the issue is "disruption." There should never be a presumption in favor of suspension or exclusion if those sanctions will effectively terminate the child's education.

These presumptions should be indulged for several reasons. First, courts and legislatures have expressed a preference for mainstreaming. Second, the presumptions advance the goals of individualized education (the educator must overcome them by showing in each case that special schooling is more appropriate for the child). Third, the presumptions suggest that new procedures, new burdens of proof, and new elements of proof should be forthcoming if the educator attempts to overcome the presumption in favor of mainstreaming.

Before proceeding further with the efforts to balance the rights and duties of the various parties, it is appropriate to discuss the nature of the due process hearing. The hearing should consist of inquiries into the interests, rights, and duties of the parties; the nature of the control exercised over the pupil by the school; the environment of the school as it affects or is affected by the pupil; and the pupil's behavior as a response to or in the school environment.

To facilitate these inquiries, the hearing, as a general rule, should be a full-fledged due process hearing, affording to the parties the entire panoply of procedural safeguards. There should be no hearing unless and until the parties can agree in advance on the meaning of the standards to be applied, i.e., unless they can agree on the meaning of the terms "emotionally disturbed" or "socially maladjusted." Without agreement on the meanings of these terms, the parties will find it difficult to determine the nature of the child's behavior; instead, they will continue to deal only with the child's behavioral symptoms and manifestations. Until they determine the cause and the nature of the child's behavior (whether he is "emotionally disturbed" or "socially maladjusted"), they will be unable to agree on the nature and extent of their rights with respect to each other and the nature and extent of any appropriate educational intervention (whether the child is to be mainstreamed or provided with special educational services).

It will be argued that classifying the child (e.g., "he is emotionally disturbed") does not necessarily suggest that special education intervention is appropriate. This is true. Conversely, it is true that classifying the child may indeed suggest that special education intervention is appropriate. In either event, classifying the child helps the parties determine the nature and extent of their respective rights and duties.

At the hearing, there should be, first, an inquiry into whether the pupil committed certain acts (his behavior) and what the educator did or did not do with respect to the behavior, and, second, whether the pupil should be held accountable for his action or excused from its consequences either because it was primarily caused by the school environment or the educator's actions or because it was substantially beyond his control (because of his emotional disabilities). The hearing thus should be designed to find facts and determine causation (who—the pupil or the school—is "at fault") and exoneration (whether the pupil's behavior is to be excused).

It will be difficult to determine causation. It may not even be desirable to do so, but it probably is necessary. The consequences of suspension or expulsion (particularly expulsion) are so grave for the student that he should have the opportunity to raise the matter of causation, if he wants. Moreover, the matter of causation directly affects decisions on teacher competency.

Finally, the hearing should inquire into the necessity for special educational intervention and, if that necessity is established, into the nature of such intervention. The severity and persistence of the child's behavior and its nature and causes may well suggest not only the nature of the special intervention but also whether sanctions (such as suspension or expulsion) should be imposed.

In inquiring into the nature and extent of special educational intervention, the preferences of the courts and legislatures for the mainstream, as well as the relative educational advantages and disadvantages of mainstreaming, suggest that the following less-to-more drastic alternative interventions are appropriate:

a. problem handled in regular class with no special intervention;
b. regular classroom placement with assistance of resource personnel (such as resource teachers, teacher aides, school psychologists, school psychiatrists, and others);

   c. regular classroom placement, supplemented by additional placement
      in special education class;
   d. part-time regular class and part-time special class;
   e. full-time special self-contained class; or
   f. total exclusion from the school environment with referral to other
      appropriate governmental or private agencies for special intervention
      and continuance of educational program.

This aspect of the hearing, of course, would be incomplete without
(1) a finding concerning the length of duration of any of the above alternatives, and (2) a provision for a regularly scheduled review of the
determination of the intervention or sanction (to allow for remission or
improvement on the pupil's part or for a change in the educational environment on the educator's part).

EFFECTS OF MAINSTREAMING

The effects of mainstreaming on the relationship of the parent and pupil,
on the one hand, and the educator, on the other, are significant. The requirement that the educator comply with procedural due process in edu
cational placement, tracking, or classification is more than a requirement
that the parent and child be given an opportunity to protest a placement
decision, as, for example, a decision to mainstream or not mainstream a
pupil. It is a tool by which mainstreaming can be achieved or resisted.
It is a mechanism for making the student the center of the educational
process and for displacing a system-centered educational process which
required the student to fit the system, rather than the system to fit him.
    While this may be an advantage, it likewise may rebound to the
pupil's disadvantage by making him the center of controversy between
the parent and the educator. If indeed it may make him the central focus
of other persons' essentially adversary relationships, then it is appropriate
to ask whether the due process hearing always should be full fledged.
The fact that adversary roles between parent and educator may be
counterproductive for the child has implications for the nature and extent
of the due process hearing. It is not farfetched to surmise that the more
formal and extensive the hearing is, the more likely it will emphasize
and possibly exacerbate the adversariness of the parent/educator relationship. If this is possible, then it is also possible that, whatever the out-

come of the hearing (whether the child is mainstreamed or not), subtle and informal sanctions may be applied to him by the educator if the educator "loses" at the hearing. It is also likely that those types of sanctions will be beyond the power of a due process hearing to reach and redress. Likewise, if the parent "loses," it is possible that he will find ways—perhaps subconsciously—for "taking it out" on the child. The risk of retribution is run almost entirely by the child when the relationship of the parent and educator is hardened into an adversary mold by the requirement of procedural due process; and the risk increases almost directly in proportion to the extent that the due process hearing is formalized and made more into an adversary, rather than conciliatory, hearing.

The requirement of procedural due process is not, however, without its advantages, including some that seem to have no counterproductive or disadvantageous aspects. Procedural due process provides both the parent and the child with a method for making the school system more accountable to them. It tends to change the parents' or child's relationship to the educator from one of passivity or acquiescence in the educator's decisions to one of active participation in and skeptical inquiry into the educational process. And it tends to demystify the educational process by providing the parent and child with an opportunity to participate in the process; it makes the relatively unknown more knowable and thus more or less acceptable. In doing so, it either gives implicit approval to the educator or withdraws the parents' and child's approval; if the former, it does not tend to excite the parent and child to action but, if the latter, it is likely to make them skeptical. In both cases, it makes the school system accountable.

The educator is effected in many of the same ways as the parent and child, and yet in different ways, too. He is obliged to comply with the rule of accountability, to adopt a cooperative and nonauthoritarian stance with respect to the parent and child, and to reconstruct the school system so that it will no longer remain system-centered but will become, instead, child-centered. More significantly, he must begin to find ways to reshape the school's environment so that it will accommodate the emotionally disturbed child, rather than reject him. Exactly how the school environment and the values of school personnel—their attitudes toward the child—are to be reshaped is less a matter for the lawyer's concern than for the educator's. Yet in insisting on the educator's compliance with the child's rights, the legal tool of due process becomes an instrument of change. It becomes a catalyst that may make the school more reflective of non-school values, may make it more accurately mirror the social values that lie behind the legal principles (the values of accommodation and acceptance of difference), and thus may impel a change in educational environment with respect to the emotionally disturbed child. In special education, the law is now acting far more as a catalyst than a mirror; it impels change rather than reinforces cultural norms—it says that rejection of emotional disturbance is to be avoided.

In addition, the educator is affected by the requirement—implicit in procedural and substantive due process—that his placement decisions be rational. Moreover, he and his system's deficiencies are liable to be exposed and magnified through the requirement of procedural due process, through the due process hearing itself.

When an inquiry is made into the school's environment through a due process hearing and the inquiry results in an attempt to reshape that environment to make it more hospitable to the emotionally disturbed student, there may be a concomitant re-evaluation of the concept of education as an acculturization and normalizing mechanism and thus a resulting re-definition of education—a re-definition that suggests abandoning the schools' normalizing role and the traditional academic curriculum. The schools may no longer be seen as having the legitimate function of shaping students to a common mold if they are required as a matter of law to accommodate the emotionally disturbed or disturbing child and thus are required as a matter of their operations and ideology to make themselves more hospitable to that child.

To accomplish these goals, the educator may be required to provide not only an academic, normalizing, and acculturalizing curriculum, but also a wider range of human services than has been provided in the past. It is conceivable, given the requirement that the educator not terminate the student's education during periods of suspension, that the educator may have to begin providing or contracting for the types of services provided by departments of social services, health, public health, and mental health. In short, in order to instruct in the traditional curriculum and further to comply with the duty of continuous education, the school may itself have to significantly supplement and diversify its services and become a human-resources agency as well as an educational agency.

Finally, if the educator is unable to reshape his system's environment, curriculum, and services to accommodate the emotionally disturbed or disturbing child, serious question arises about the wisdom of the school compulsory attendance laws. If the school environment is damaging to some students, and if the school is unable to change its environment so that it does less or minimal damage to them, it subjects them to the risk of damage if they are required under the school compulsory attendance laws to continue to attend school. To suggest that exceptions should be made to the compulsory attendance laws may seem to be contrary to the doctrine that a child has a constitutional right to education, and indeed the suggestion may be contrary to that doctrine unless alternative systems of education are developed. But education does not have to be limited to schooling in the school building itself. It may encompass competency-based training that has little to do with traditional academic or vocational education. Within competency-based training, it may include types of training in self-development that may well be far outside the realm of what presently is in the educator's curriculum. Alternative systems for developing the student's capacities may be the ultimate outcome of the legal requirements of individualized and child-centered training and of the requirements of accommodation of differences.

FINANCING IMPLICATIONS

In shaping the school system to fit the student, the law engages in a traditional role of institutional reform and rebuilding. Several aspects of the institutional reform merit special mention. Financing is one of them.

The requirements that will be made on local school systems as a result of mainstreaming emotionally disturbed students or reconstructing the school's abilities and responsibilities to deal with them carry accompanying demands on the local level of school financing and thus have implications for the pattern of school financing. If the fiscal demands outstrip the ability of local school systems to respond, a shift in the pattern of financing from primarily local to primarily state financing may occur. It need not, however, necessitate a similar centralizing shift in planning and program development, which may nevertheless retain local characteristics under a state-level financing scheme. Local planning and program responsibility will, however, begin to yield to state-level planning and programming if local schools are neither able nor willing to comply with the new requirements for mainstreaming or providing educational alternatives to the emotionally disturbed student. That would be unfortunate if it also heralds the abandonment of small school units, where mainstreaming may be more feasible than in larger ones. Fiscal centralization does not have to entail administrative centralization.

Another fiscal dislocation may be in the offing. Equal protection in the provision of educational services is a cornerstone principle in opening up the school system to the emotionally disturbed or disturbing child; it also is a principle that advances the interests of mainstreaming. Yet it is a two-edged sword. It asserts equality in access to education, but it likewise arguably asserts that special consideration to special education is impermissible, with the possibly untoward consequence that programs for the emotionally disturbed student, which presumably cost more to operate per capita than programs for the "normal" student, may be limited to per capita expenditures equal to those for "normal" or "regular" education programs. This result would be unfortunate in the case of the more generously financed programs for the special student but a boon for the less-than-equally financed programs. Principles of equality may impinge upon or enhance the special education of one category of special student where the equality must exist with respect to that special child and the "normal" child. It also may have similar consequences if equality means that equal expenditures per capita or per type of special student is to be required among the various categories of special children. For example, expenditures on the emotionally disturbed must equal expenditures on the mentally retarded.

Implicit in these considerations is the issue whether funds that ordinarily would be spent for special education of the emotionally disturbed may be diverted from their original purpose in order to be spent on the costs of mainstreaming the emotionally disturbed, that is, on enabling not only the emotionally disturbed to cope with the mainstream but on enabling the mainstream to cope with the child. Also implicit is the issue that categorical programs for different types of special students may be necessary since they assure that funds and programs will reach the types of special students who need special help, but undesirable because of their tendency to resist mainstreaming efforts, among other reasons.

CLOUT

Another change in school institutions that may result from mainstreaming is the enhancement of special education itself through additions to its presently limited financial manpower and political resources. These changes may occur because special education will come to be seen as a preparatory curriculum for mainstreaming instead of as a terminal placement for the emotionally disturbed child. If the lawmaker's policy preference for mainstreaming overrides a traditional preference for separate special education, special education may take on additional importance and thus clout, since it will be seen as a necessary tributary into the mainstream, not as a separate and parallel river.

MANPOWER IMPLICATIONS

The third and final institution-shaping aspect of mainstreaming involves personnel matters. Two in particular are of special legal concern. The requirement for mainstreaming raises the issue of teacher competency: is the teacher competent to deal with the mainstreamed emotionally disturbed student? If not, under what circumstances, if any, can or should the teacher be relieved of the requirement of having emotionally disturbed students mainstreamed into his or her class? Or, should the question more properly be whether and, if so, under what circumstances the student should be relieved of the burden of the incompetent teacher into whose classroom he is mainstreamed?

When the issue of teacher competence is considered in the legal framework of relief for one person, the teacher, or another, the pupil, the teacher usually has been granted relief in the exclusion of the child from the teacher's classroom and thus from mainstream education. This result is consistent not only with system-centered education but with the many legally sanctioned protections of teachers, including the tenure system.

Yet, if the focus in education is to be on the pupil, not the system and the teachers who are parts of that system, the result may have to favor the pupil. Such a change would have obvious and serious implications for teacher tenure rules. The change would put the burden on the school and the teacher to justify a pupil's exclusion from the mainstream and would require the school and the teacher to demonstrate that exclusion from the mainstream is in the student's best educational interests, notwithstanding the policy preference for mainstreaming. If, as part of the due process hearing (the inquiry into causation and exoneration) at which this proof would have to be adduced, the student can show that the school and teacher are more "at fault" than he, then the school would not have successfully discharged its burden; indeed, the child would have shown not only that the school and the teacher are "at fault," but he would have raised a strong suggestion that the teacher (not the pupil) should be removed from the system.

In short, if the teacher proves to be incompetent to handle mainstreaming, should the teacher be removed from the system, and, if so, what are the consequences of an affirmative decision on this question for teacher tenure regulations? Or, is it even necessary to reach the tenure issue at the outset? Could a less drastic inquiry be just as appropriate; namely, should a new set of rules be developed for teacher reassignment, suspension, or exclusion where the teacher proves to be incompetent to handle mainstreaming, where the teacher is found to be the catalyst in the child's behavior, or where the teacher violates the student's legal rights (to be mainstreamed and to receive an appropriate education)? What is to be the most satisfactory method for handling teacher-union contract provisions that safeguard the teachers against having to teach in "mainstreamed" classes? These are necessary but difficult questions. They beg answers that are beyond the scope of this article and, perhaps, our present experience.

CONCLUSION

Lawmaking has never been a facile process. It is the result of balancing many competing rights, duties, interests, claims, and aspirations. As Paul aptly indicates in Chapter 1, the lawmaker runs the risk of losing perspective on the implications of mainstreaming and of creating a tidal wave of changes that may have undesirable institutional effects. It is against this risk that procedural due process stands as the best safeguard. Due process requires not only a balancing of interests and thus their resolution, but it also points the way toward the policy that lawmakers can adopt without accompanying institutional damage: the policy of child-centered, individualized education. Due process guarantees at least a fair procedure in education; it thus may make more acceptable the results that flow from the procedure. Other contributors to this book have indicated, far better than a lawyer might, how the education of the emotionally disturbed child can be individualized. They have indicated the direction for the policy.

It is a mistake to place too much reliance on the legal process—on the judgment of courts, the wisdom of legislators, the advocacy skills of attorneys, and the fairness of procedures. Almost every social and political issue of our times inevitably has become a legal and constitutional issue. The winds of social and political change blow through the court-house and the legislative halls only shortly after they affect the atmos-phere of social institutions, especially the schools.

In dealing with the disturbance caused by the winds of change, the lawmaker necessarily moves slowly. If he is to accommodate them, he must necessarily affect social institutions. As a judge, he makes change, through case law, incrementally; as a legislator, he makes change, through statutes, both incrementally and sweepingly. But all of these changes are often slow to seep into and change the lattices of social in-stitutions. Bureaucracy—especially school bureaucracy—may be par-ticularly impermeable to the lawmaker's requirement of change. If it is, then the importance of mainstreaming a system, through the many de-vices suggested in other chapters in this book, becomes the lawmaker's hope. He has his role, but he must rely on his fellow players. To see the lawmaker as the central figure in the play is to misconceive the nature of the drama of change.

AFTERWORD

One of the most difficult tasks for commentators on the law is to keep their published material up to date with current events. That problem is illustrated by the fact that this chapter was prepared prior to the enact-ment of P.L. 94-142 ("Education of All Handicapped Children Act"). Happily, many of the arguments advanced in the paper are reflected in that significant federal statute.

For example, P.L. 94-142 provides that the parents or guardian of a handicapped child (the term "handicapped child" includes the emo-tionally disturbed child) or the child per se have procedural due process rights, including the right to notice and an opportunity for a hearing on the issues of the identification, evaluation, or placement of the child or on the issue of the educator's responsibility to provide each pupil with a free appropriate public education. The due process safeguards also in-clude a right to access to the records, to counsel, to a hearing before an impartial hearing officer, to examine and cross-examine witnesses, to an independent education evaluation, to multidisciplinary evaluations, to a written record of the hearing and a written order setting out the findings of fact and order of the hearing officer, to administrative and judicial appeals, and to remain in the original placement unless an alternative placement is agreeable to the parents or guardian.

Moreover, P.L. 94-142 establishes a policy of zero-reject, prohibiting a school from excluding any child because of his handicap. This policy means, and P.L. 94-142 contemplates, that homebound, institutionalized, hospitalized and private-school educated children will receive the same rights as children in the public schools.

Significantly, P.L. 94-142 also establishes a policy in favor of an educational placement in the least restrictive alternative placement commensurate with the child's needs and abilities. Thus, it opts for a policy of appropriate education with a bias for mainstream education.

Finally, it requires that each handicapped child be furnished an individualized education plan. Parents and the child are to be included with educators in the development of that plan, and the plan is to be reviewed annually and revised when appropriate.

REFERENCES

Goss vs. Lopez (49 U.S. 565, 43 L.W. 4181, 1975).

Kirp, D.; Buss, W.; & Kuriloff, P. *Legal Reform of Special Education: Empirical Studies and Procedural Proposals. 62 Cal. L. Rev. 40* (1974).

McClung, M. *The Problem of Due Process Exclusion. 3 Jour. of Law and Education 491* (1974).

Weintraub, F. and Abeson, A. *Appropriate Education for All Handicapped Children: A Growing Issue. 23 Syracuse L. Rev. 1037* (1972).

5

Human Understanding
of Human Behavior

RICHARD J. WHELAN

IT HAS ONLY BEEN WITHIN the last two decades that educational services for children with learning and behavior disorders (the emotionally disturbed) have been recognized as an integral portion of therapeutic intervention strategies (Hirschberg 1953). The roots of educators' inclusion within the traditional treatment team of the psychiatrist, clinical psychologist, and psychiatric social worker were first identifiable in residential treatment centers. Pioneer educators (Haring and Phillips 1962; Long, Morse, and Newman 1965; Redl and Wineman 1957) used the knowledge learned in residential facilities to develop special learning programs for emotionally disturbed children who were placed in day and public school facilities.

As the role of educators in the treatment of emotionally disturbed children was accepted by mental health professionals, and as that role became more focused, the number and types of educational models to serve children increased (Morse, Cutler, and Fink 1964; Whelan 1966). In addition, model-specific personnel preparation programs for the emotionally disturbed were developed to meet the need for more qualified educators. The recent increase in teacher preparation programs was largely due to the professional and financial stimulation of federal agencies, specifically, the Division of Personnel Preparation, Bureau of Education for the Handicapped, United States Office of Education. A reciprocal effect was observed because of the federal stimulus. The number of educational programs for children expanded, thus creating a demand for more teachers. As the teacher supply increased, more agencies, particularly the public schools, initiated new service programs. Most of these programs followed the special class model, but Morse's (1965) concept of the "crisis teacher" was an exception to the general trend. The "crisis teacher" often functioned in a public school facility to provide consultant services to regular class teachers, and to interact on an individual basis with a child or with small groups of children who displayed observable academic and social behavior deficits and excesses. As such, the "crisis teacher" model is the antecedent for the rather recent development of using consultant teachers to provide services rather than relying solely upon the self-contained, special class teacher.

While the growth in the number of educational programs for the emotionally disturbed is impressive, it is estimated by the Bureau of Education for the Handicapped that at least 75 percent of these children are not receiving appropriate educational services. This estimate is based upon a 2 percent prevalence figure which is very conservative when compared with the 10 percent estimate cited by Bower (1960).

What is to be done for, to, or with this unserved group of children, and who should be involved in the doing? The special class model is no more the solution of choice any more than residential treatment is, or any other of the more recent models currently being initiated in public schools. Obviously, a wide range of educational service programs must be provided by the special educator. The programs must be designed to serve the unique, diverse learning styles of children, the *sine qua non* of education. To meet this challenge, educators will need to resist the temptation of grouping children on the basis of noneducational information, affixing a label to the grouping, and only then attempting to plan learning experiences for what is thought to be a homogenous group, but which is, in reality, a nonfunctional educational mix.

Even if a full range of educational services could be provided by public school special educators, would the needs of the child called "emotionally disturbed" be served? Probably not, since need expands in relationship to supply. That is, when more professionals are available, the needs increase to the point where even more professionals must be supplied. Carrying this logic to the extreme, and without considering economic restrictions, would result in the schools' being totally staffed by special educators. If this situation were to occur, it can be anticipated that a new, even more specialized group would arise to serve the "fallout" children who would not respond to the new order of instruction. The historical cycle would be repeated again, and again, *ad infinitum*.

No, there must be other alternatives to the proliferation of educational specialists. On economic grounds alone, continued specialization cannot be supported. More importantly, further professional specialization should not be supported at a philosophical level. After all, it is the positive interaction between pupil and teacher over time that strengthens a relationship which is, in turn, fundamental to pupil behavior change. Good teaching fosters a positive relationship, and a child's life is enhanced from it. Further fragmentation of pupils' contact with an identifiable "my teacher" would obviate the possibility of establishing a facilitative learner-teacher relationship. A pupil would be left with a sequence of task points at which information would be exchanged, deleted, and added much like a machine is kept running, and all of this would be done with the attendant lack of interpersonal relationships.

One realistic and desirable alternative to the expansion of special programs is to use the expertise of the so-called regular educator in providing instruction for children who are, or may become, members of a group labeled emotionally disturbed. Many of these children are now in regular public school classes. They display a wide variance of behavior ranging from academic failure to just barely making it, and from obviously aggressive acts to almost total withdrawal. The teachers and children feel frustrated, defeated, and hopeless in finding alternative ways of building facilitative interpersonal relationships. Yet, these children have been and remain "mainstreamed," and it is likely that they will continue to be so in the future. This status need not have a negative impact *if* regular educators can receive the preparation and external support necessary to enable them to plan learning environments facilitative of positive pupil development in academic and social behaviors. The external support in the areas of curriculum, classroom management, and parent programs can be provided by personnel who are called "consultant teachers," "crisis teachers," or "resource room teachers." This extra support can take the form of direct contact with pupils and/or interaction with teachers only. Still, the major impact of providing quality educational experiences resides with regular class teachers, the ones who interact with children five hours a day. Therefore, this group will need additional preparation in instructional procedures and behavior management approaches.

Providing the additional preparation in the pedagogy of special education will require financial resources and administrative support at all levels of the educational system. Yet, something more, and probably even more important, is needed before presently mainstreamed emotionally disturbed can begin to benefit and progress in regular education settings. Martin (1974) has stated this "something more" quite well; attention must be given to understanding and changing the fears and misconceptions that regular educators have developed because of the general society's attitudes toward those who are different. Special educators must change too. They must learn to appreciate and understand the unique problems regular educators have in devising individualized instructional programs in a large group setting. In short, both regular and special educators will need to use effective communication and concerted action in developing learning experiences for children in regular classrooms who are different, such as the emotionally disturbed. What educators do to or for children must evolve out of what is needed by children. To do this requires total professional and personal commitment to the provision of quality education for all children.

FOCUS AND PURPOSE

This chapter describes a system which educators can use in understanding self and others' behavior reactions to situations. The system is far too simplistic to totally explain the occurrence of behavior which is often complex in topography and function. However, if the system described here adds even minimal clarity and insight for understanding behavior, it will have served a useful purpose. More importantly, it may stimulate further thinking and analysis by dedicated educators.

The author owes a great deal of gratitude to Dr. Nicholas J. Long, a pioneer educator of emotionally disturbed children. Many years ago, at a mental health meeting in Kansas City, Missouri, Long presented a model for understanding the deviant behavior of emotionally disturbed children. That model was known as the conflict cycle. A revised version of the model was published by Long in 1974. Long's model functioned to stimulate this author to think and work toward additional insights into the understanding of human behavior. While Long's model provides a systematic approach to the understanding of deviant behavior, it does not account for the occurrence of those behaviors which are positive, productive, and growth oriented. Therefore, the system described in this chapter was designed to elicit understanding of both deviant and positive behavior as they occur in school situations, a necessary condition for a system or model to meet if it is to have utility and if it is to function as an aid in improving instructional practices in learning environments.

A school is responsible for providing academic and social-growth producing experiences for the pupils enrolled. Pupils attend school for many reasons, and it is necessary that staff recognize and relate to these wide variations in student motivation and behavior. Whether the reason for attendance is positive, negative, or a combination of both, the staff has the responsibility for assisting pupils to develop to maximum capability. It is not necessary to point out the immenseness and difficulty of this task; most educators are quite aware of it. Yet, it is important to recognize what a new pupil encounters upon arriving at the school. Subsequent portions of this chapter describe a rationale for understanding the behavior of others and that exhibited by oneself. Understanding behavior is the basis upon which programs are developed to bring about positive changes in behavior. It is only through human to human interaction as it occurs in learning environments that behavior can be understood and changed.

HUMAN ENVIRONMENT INTERACTION

Human to human interaction can be described as any contact between or among individuals that leads to some type of communication. The communication can be conversational (verbal), or it can be facial expressions and body movements (nonverbal). The situation in which this communication takes place is referred to as the environment. An environment may be a classroom, playground, lunch room, office, or school bus.

Staff members at a school are responsible for providing facilitative learning environments. This means that educators design an interaction process which functions to change behavior. Changing behavior can be viewed as a rather global goal of the school. That is, there should be noticeable changes in pupil behavior when comparisons are made between entering and departing behavior. It is not only pupil behavior that is changed. Staff behavior and understanding of behavior should also change as a result of pupil-staff interaction. The term "facilitative" is used to convey the notion that pupil-staff interactions must be planned to achieve positive and successful growth-producing experiences. If a learning environment does not provide for such positive encounters, then it is not facilitating desirable and realistic behavior change.

It is important that staff members recognize the fear or tenseness which a pupil may feel, but not necessarily show, upon entering a new school situation. Because the situation is new, the pupil cannot know or predict what will be encountered or what will be expected in terms of behavior. The pupil may have come from a situation in which relationships were confined to very few people. However, at a school the pupil must learn to relate to many individuals who have many different roles. A first difficult task is to learn: "Who to go to for what. . . . Who is seen about class schedules. . . . Whom do I ask for permission to call home?" To understand the complexity of a school operation, particularly as it must appear to a new pupil, one has only to list the names of staff and positions. The list will contain positions for cooks, maintenance people, principal, teachers, counselors, nurse, secretary, etc. In addition, the new pupil must come to know fellow pupils. Learning and sorting out all of this information is difficult, and the new pupil will encounter feelings of loneliness, sadness, uncertainty, and fear until some comfort is obtained through adjustment over time. If staff members are aware of these initial factors, the pupil's behavior reactions to the new situation can be understood, and assistance can be provided to enhance situational adjustment.

A school and its staff may be the first totally organized institution that a child encounters. The school is designed to provide daily guidance and opportunities for learning. It must function to change human behavior in a manner that will enable individuals to procure the responsibilities and benefits that society offers. It enables individuals to acquire the competencies that are necessary for continual success and growth in daily living ventures. When children leave a familiar situation such as the home to enter a school, they are expected to accomplish three objectives:

1. Leave a familiar situation, whether it may have been negative or positive, and venture into relatively unknown, uncertain areas of expectations for behavior performances.

2. Establish a new set of interpersonal relationships with peers and adults.

3. Acquire and accumulate skills and knowledge which will culminate in behaviors that are necessary for becoming a contributing member of society.

For some individuals, attaining these objectives means a change from various stages of dependent, unsocialized, self-centered behaviors to points upon the behavior continuum which represent degrees of independent, socialized, and group-centered behavior.

To enable an individual to accomplish the three objectives, a school must plan facilitative learning environments (FLE) (Whelan 1972). FLEs represent a basic philosophical position that should enable school staff to assist pupils in attaining desirable and realistic objectives. They provide the foundation upon which specific, detailed interpersonal interactions are planned, implemented, and evaluated. FLEs are designed to assist staff and pupils in organizing programs which can systematically provide services based upon individual pupil needs or unique learning requirements. These programs are devised to provide functional assistance and service for pupils who have not progressed as anticipated in areas of academic or social behavior development within prior learning environments. Such programs plan FLEs for individuals whose behavior growth has been limited by the nature of past and present learning environments in which they have been expected to function.

The provision and implementation of FLEs for an individual or a group are based upon the rationale that behavior progress has not been facilitated by past or present assignment to a specific and identifiable learning environment. That is, the human-to-human learning environment interaction has not operated in a manner that promotes expected and identifiable progress. As a result of inappropriate interaction, an individual may exhibit *behavior excesses* (fighting) and *behavior deficits* (not finishing school assignments). An individual may be said to have a behavior excess if exhibited behaviors are not desirable or beneficial to the individual or to others. The individual exhibits too many of those behaviors that should not be displayed. A deficit is a behavior that the individual should exhibit but does not, or does not at the right time and place. FLEs should implement changes in the environment that will reduce behavior excesses and promote the learning of behaviors that will decrease behavior deficits.

It is important and necessary to understand how maladaptive behavior excesses and deficits can occur. Of equal importance is the understanding of how adaptive or successful behavior patterns are learned. If it is true that behavior is learned, then learning principles should apply equally to the understanding of how maladaptive as well as adaptive behaviors are developed. Figure 5.1 is a simplified schematic of a model or cycle for understanding why behavior patterns occur in a variety of situations. Each component of the cycle is described and discussed in subsequent sections of the chapter. Arrows indicate the sequential relationship between and among the various components of the cycle.

BEFORE SCHOOL PRIOR ENVIRONMENTAL EXPERIENCES AND INDIVIDUAL (SELF) EVALUATION

Previous portions of this chapter mentioned the variations of prior environmental experiences that an individual may encounter before attend-

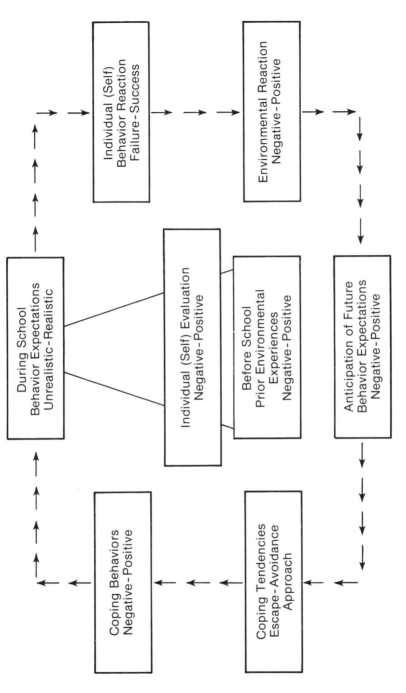

FIGURE 5.1. Behavior excess, deficit and adaptation cycle.

ing a school. These prior experiences have a profound effect upon the manner in which an individual enters into a new learning environment. This effect is visually indicated by the placement of these two variables at the center of the cycle. Prior experiences permeate and influence to a significant degree those behavior patterns which will occur in the future. For example, if a pupil has experienced more failure than success in school tasks, a new school situation will be viewed with suspicion and caution. The pupil may say, "Nobody has cared whether I do well or not, so why should I trust these people?" Even though the school staff may be most understanding and knowledgeable about previous problems, the pupil will still approach them with attitudes formed by previous experiences. The pupil may have been hurt or let down by others when trust was given. This past history will affect the pupil's style in interacting with teachers and others. Time, patience, and understanding on the part of staff would be needed before the pupil could trust in others again.

Past experiences affect how an individual feels about himself. If asked to evaluate himself, the individual may say "I am perfect," or "I don't have any problems at all." Both of these self-evaluations should be questioned; they are not realistic. Nevertheless, because of a history of failure, an individual may have a self-evaluation that is quite negative: "If I can't do anything right, then I must be bad." The individual may not say this directly, but it can be observed in behavior patterns displayed in school or at home. Other individuals, who feel that they are perfect, seem to be confident, and will not learn from others often use this type of behavior to cover up true feelings of inadequacy. It is a front which disguises the fact that they really feel quite inadequate. An understanding staff can observe and identify this behavior pattern. The self-confident behavior is too fragile; it is not believable. The individual is not as skilled as verbal statements would indicate, and this discrepancy is easily observed. Once the false front is removed, the individual can be assisted to acquire adaptive and successful styles of behavior.

It is important to recognize that the front cannot be removed by simply telling the individual "You are covering up an essentially negative self-evaluation." To take this approach would only produce intensified reactions to keep up the false front, and would only confirm the individual's assertions that others cannot be trusted. Rather, the front is removed, over time, as a product of functional interpersonal interactions with staff. The individual learns and acquires insight which illustrates that it is possible to succeed in meeting behavior expectations. In time, and with a series of many successes, the individual will lose the behavior façade and will be able to place trust in others. Self-evaluation will become more realistic in that individual strengths and weaknesses are recognized. As the individual achieves success in meeting daily responsibilities, personal adjustment will improve. To make an error will not mean that the individual is all bad. Because of many prior successes, the error is recognized and procedures to correct it are instituted. The error is not viewed as a negative self-evaluation; instead, it is seen as another opportunity to attain a successful solution of a problem.

DURING SCHOOL BEHAVIOR EXPECTATIONS

When a pupil first enters school, it is necessary to learn what is expected in class, the cafeteria, and many other situations. Staff members should have as much information as possible about the pupil's past experiences and methods of evaluating the self. This information should be used to devise realistic behavior expectations for the pupil. If expectations are unrealistic, a previous failure history or cycle will be continued. If this occurs, the pupil's chances of changing behavior would be significantly reduced.

Knowing what or when a behavior expectation is correct is a difficult task. Errors will be made, but if staff members are aware of how a pupil reacts when faced with an expectation to behave in a certain manner, such errors can be kept at a minimum. Careful observation of the individual pupil can assist the staff in determining sequential and realistic behavior expectations.

INDIVIDUAL (SELF) BEHAVIOR REACTION

When confronted with a behavior expectation, an individual will respond or react. If the reaction is correct, the individual knows and feels success in accomplishing a task. The task may be a math page or an assignment to bring in playground equipment. If the individual cannot complete the math assignment because it is beyond what was learned in other math classes, failure occurs, and the individual recognizes or is aware of this event.

The manner or way in which a pupil reacts is also valuable information for the staff. If the math assignment is too difficult, it can be withdrawn and a new one presented. By observing pupil reaction, the staff can become more accurate in presenting realistic and appropriate behavior expectations.

ENVIRONMENTAL REACTION

A behavior reaction is followed by an environmental reaction. If the pupil completes the math assignment in an acceptable manner (a passing grade), the teacher may verbally remark that the pupil did very well. This subsequent environmental reaction is important, particularly if teacher comments and recognition are valued by the pupil. For example, if teacher praise has great value, a pupil will strive to obtain it. A pupil who has experienced past failure in math may see no intrinsic merit in doing math problems. However, if by doing them, the teacher's praise results, correct math tasks will become more frequent. In time, the pupil begins to learn the value of completing a task, and teacher praise may lose some of its importance. The pupil attains self-satisfaction from having solved a problem. This example applies to all staff. There are many situations in a school where recognition of a task well done can be used to assist pupils to acquire adaptive behavior patterns. Keeping a neat desk, finishing reading before going to recess, etc., are examples of student behavior that can be recognized and commented upon by staff members.

The environmental reaction can also be applied by peers as well as staff, as when the peer group also praises the successful completion of a task. However, it must be recognized that the peer group may have a negative reaction to behaviors that the staff believes deserves a positive reaction. It can be seen that the pupil could be placed in a conflict situation. If the peer group influence is stronger than that of the staff members, the pupil will probably behave in the fashion expected by his peers. These situations are very complex, and correcting them is beyond the intent or scope of this brief chapter. The obvious solution is for the staff to enlist the peer group as helpers to assist in obtaining behavior change. For instance, in a small instructional group of five or six pupils, the staff can plan certain events and tasks. When all tasks are completed by all the individuals, then the group may engage in other activities such as art or music. If the peer group is aware of this arrangement, members can assist each other in successful completion of assigned tasks. In this manner, a cooperative rather than competitive group interaction is encouraged. As indicated previously, these situations are quite complex, and efforts to use peer influence can fail if not arranged correctly. Harsh physical punishment of an individual by the peer group can occur; obviously this is neither positive nor warranted. It is suggested that the staff conduct detailed studies of group interaction principles before implementing peer group behavior change plans. The basic principles of behavior change are few in number and relatively simple, but their correct implementation can be very complicated.

If a pupil fails to complete a math assignment, the environmental reaction will probably be negative. The teacher may place a low grade on the assignment or may verbally admonish the pupil. For a pupil who desires teacher praise, a reprimand may motivate more careful preparation of future assignments in order to obtain teacher recognition. A pupil who fails many assignments may view the negative environmental reaction as one more piece of evidence to confirm a poor or low self-evaluation.

Positive environmental reactions function to promote the acquisition of desirable adaptive behaviors. Negative environmental reactions usually decrease the frequency of maladaptive behaviors. These are general behavior principles, but specific application to individuals requires a great deal of competence and skill. To some individuals, verbal praise or reprimands mean nothing; they do not function as reactions that change behavior. In these instances more concrete environmental reactions such as completing tasks to earn certain privileges, always accompanied by verbal praise for a successful task completion, can be applied. In time, the association of the concrete reaction with the verbal reaction can enhance the power of verbal recognition by others to foster behavior change; the concrete reactions gradually lose some of their importance as positive human-to-human interaction becomes more frequent.

Staff members can observe which types of environmental reactions are effective in changing pupil behavior. Careful observation of these effects should enable the staff to plan reactions that will assist pupils meet behavior expectations successfully.

ANTICIPATION OF FUTURE BEHAVIOR EXPECTATIONS

When an individual fails to attain a behavior expectation and, as a result, receives a negative environmental reaction, it is reasonable to assume that the individual would not strive to enter into a similar situation in the future. This anticipation or dread about future events can be seen in fear, tenseness, and anxiety. More precisely, the condition of anxiety may be described as the anticipation of negative, aversive, or punishing environmental reactions.

For the individual who has attained success in accomplishing behavior expectations, plus positive environmental reactions, it is reasonable to assume that the individual will strive to enter similar situations in the future. Such anticipation may be described by such terms as "happy" or "joyful." A happy behavior condition may be defined as the anticipation of positive, pleasurable, or rewarding environmental reactions.

Anticipation, whether negative or positive, of future behavior expectations is an important aspect in developing and understanding behavior. If a pupil has experienced many failures, it is difficult for the staff to plan behavior expectations that might result in successful completion, but it must be done if a failure cycle is to be interrupted. A positive anticipation for future situations is learned because of past successes in achieving behavior expectations.

COPING TENDENCIES

Negative anticipation of subsequent behavior expectations evokes escape and avoidance tendencies within an individual who experiences repeated failure in accomplishing behavior expectations. Positive anticipation, in contrast, evokes tendencies to approach situations similar to the ones in which success has been achieved. Coping tendencies function as a type of pre-planning to escape-avoid or to approach situations that have known behavior expectations. An individual may be unaware that such planning is occurring. That is, if asked for a verbal explanation of thoughts, the individual probably could not verbalize an accurate account of these tendencies. However, skilled staff members can look for clues in an individual's behavior that will provide evidence that pre-planning is an active process.

For example, an individual may decide, though not aware that a clear decision has been made, to deny that a teacher conveyed an expectation to be at a certain place at a certain time. The denial is an example of a tendency to avoid what is thought to be a negative situation.

In this manner others can be blamed for the problem; the individual does not accept personal responsibility for self-behavior. For the individual who desires to approach a situation, any uncertainty about a behavior expectation is clarified by asking, for instance, teachers to repeat the expectation. The individual does not seize upon the opportunity to use denial and thus accepts personal responsibility for self-behavior.

COPING BEHAVIORS

The utilization of coping tendencies can be verified by careful observation of coping behaviors. As a function of pre-planning tendencies, an individual devises an array of coping behaviors that can be used in meeting behavior expectations.

If the coping tendencies are basically of an escape-avoidance nature, then the coping behaviors will be of this type—negative. For instance, complaints that the behavior expectation is unfair or too hard are often used. An individual may attempt to get a teacher sidetracked to another topic or may even disrupt the class in an attempt to avoid the behavior expectation. Or, in another situation, the individual may attempt to enlist peer group support to challenge realistic behavior expectations. Many behavior excesses and deficits are, in reality, variations of escape-avoidance coping behaviors.

The individual who has been successful in meeting most past behavior expectations will strive to learn new and positive methods of meeting future behavior expectations. This individual will strive to approach new or future behavior expectations, and, as a result, will learn alternative methods to solve problems or behavior expectations.

CONCLUSIONS

The processes described in Figure 5.1 should provide some clarification regarding human understanding of human behavior. The cycle was presented visually in order to specify that adaptive and maladaptive behavior development can be understood as emanating from the same basic behavior principles. As individuals interact with the environment, and as a function of that interaction, behavior does occur.

Facilitative learning environments emphasize the success, positive, and approach aspects of the cycle. Staff in a school are expected to plan such environments for pupils. Stress should be placed upon developing positive, successful behavior patterns. When failure, negative, and escape-avoidance aspects of the cycle are operating, staff members must attempt to shift their efforts, and the pupil's efforts, toward the positive portions of the cycle.

While the cycle can assist in understanding the occurrence of human behavior, it must be asserted that behavior is a complex process. Simple guidelines for understanding all behaviors are not available. Though some parts of this chapter provided examples of using understanding for the process of changing behavior, it should be discerned that actual procedures which can be used to change behavior are essentially a separate and independent topic for intensive analysis and study. Human understanding of human behavior is a necessary first step in designing facilitative learning environments, but additional steps must be taken before the design is complete. This chapter, it is hoped, will stimulate all staff in schools to take the additional steps and thus improve that which is provided for pupils. Not only will pupils benefit from such labors, but the staff, as a result of these labors, will benefit also. Recognition of mutually beneficial results from combined, concerted, student-staff efforts is one piece of evidence that can be used to verify that human understanding of human behavior has been achieved.

REFERENCES

Bower, E. M. *Early Identification of Emotionally Handicapped Children in Schools.* Springfield, Ill.: Thomas, 1960.

Haring, N. G., and Phillips, E. L. *Educating Emotionally Disturbed Children.* New York: McGraw-Hill, 1962.

Hirschberg, J. C. "The Role of Education in the Treatment of Emotionally Disturbed Children through Planned Ego Development." *American Journal of Orthopsychiatry* 23 (1953): 684–90.

Long, N. J. "Personal Perspectives." In *Teaching Children with Behavior Disorders,* edited by J. M. Kauffman and C. D. Lewis. Columbus, Ohio: Merrill, 1974.

————; Morse, W. C.; and Newman, R. G., eds. *Conflict in the Classroom: The Education of Emotionally Disturbed Children.* Belmont, Calif.: Wadsworth, 1965.

Martin, E. W. "Some Thoughts on Mainstreaming." *Exceptional Children* 41 (1974): 150–53.

Morse, W. C. "The Crisis Teacher." In *Conflict in the Classroom: The Education of Emotionally Disturbed Children,* edited by N. J. Long, W. C. Morse, and R. G. Newman. Belmont, Calif.: Wadsworth, 1965.

————; Cutler, R. L.; and Fink, A. H. *Public School Classes for the Emotionally Handicapped: A Research Analysis.* Washington, D.C.: Council for Exceptional Children, 1964.

Redl, F., and Wineman, D. *The Aggressive Child.* New York: Glencoe Free Press, 1957.

Whelan, R. J. "The Relevance of Behavior Modification Procedures for Teachers of Emotionally Disturbed Children." In *Intervention Approaches in Educating Emotionally Disturbed Children,* edited by P. Knoblock. Syracuse, N.Y.: Syracuse University, 1966.

————. "What's in a Label? A Hell of a Lot!" In *The Legal and Educational Consequences of the Intelligence Testing Movement: Handicapped and Minority Group Children,* edited by R. Harth, E. Meyen, and G. Nelson. Columbia: University of Missouri, 1972.

6

The Orchestration of Success

FRANK M. HEWETT

A STUDENT IN A CLASS OF MINE asked to see me in my office. She was interested, she said, in discussing a current phenomenon she understood was happening on a national basis in special education. "I think it's called, 'streamlining,' " she said. I looked puzzled. "No, maybe it's 'mainlining,' " she added. I smiled and said, "I'll bet you mean 'mainstreaming.' " And indeed she had. This humorous interaction actually is more telling than it first might appear. As we find ourselves caught up in the middle of mainstreaming, many educators, both special and regular, may well be equally as confused with respect to what this current phenomenon actually means.

Basically, the mainstreaming movement aims at guaranteeing all exceptional children, including the disturbing and disturbed child, the *right* to a public school education and the *opportunity* for a better education than many of them may now be receiving. It is the latter with which I am particularly concerned. For, if broadening and normalizing the disturbed child's educational experience through involvement with the regular education program actually does not provide a better education, then we are hardly making progress.

There are many unanswered questions still to be pondered regarding the effects of mainstreaming. Exactly what does a regular classroom have to offer the disturbed child? What are the likely positive and negative effects of integration on the child? What about the other children? Will they gain or lose in relation to their rights for a good education? And the regular teachers? How ready are they to extend their ranges of tolerance for academic and behavioral differences in the classroom which will be required if the mainstreaming process is to be successful?

These are only a few of the issues which must be dealt with as mainstreaming is implemented. Of particular concern are the first and second questions related to creating a favorable educational experience for the disturbed child who is mainstreamed.

I believe that for a favorable educational experience to occur for disturbed children a great deal of effort must go into orchestrating their success in the regular classroom. Next to "individualizing instruction," "guaranteeing success" is the most frequent definition of what special education is all about. It is an objective that is difficult to challenge. Special educators, working with disturbed children from psychodynamic, humanistic, biophysical, or behavioral points of view, find individualized instruction and the guarantee of success for the child common to each of their approaches. How much environmentally determined versus child-determined emphasis is involved in attempting to provide such individualization and success tends to separate the points of view operationally. Skinner (1972) clearly states the case for success as a powerful reinforcement in a manner difficult to argue with whatever your orientation toward the disturbed child:

> Some whopping new reinforcer is not the critical addition to the teaching act. The usual reinforcers, if used well and frequently enough, will be effective. The point of a good program is not to lead the student to obtain a very large, novel, or powerful reinforcer, but to provide reinforcement many times through his being successful again and again. The human organism, fortunately for us all, is reinforced just by being successful. Consequently, if material is designed to facilitate correct responses, the resulting frequent success is enough reinforcement for most persons. Not only will the child's behavior change as he learns to do things he could not do before, but he will become highly motivated, his morale will improve, and his attitude toward teachers will change. At this point the major effect has been achieved. Most probably teaching can be so designed that a child is reinforced simply and primarily by being successful, but this calls for precise and expert arrangements of conditions. (pp. 10–11)

How can we go about orchestrating success for the disturbed child who is mainstreamed into a regular classroom? Before dealing with the question, there is a particular issue that merits consideration. What is so good about the typical American public school classroom that justifies our moving the disturbed child toward meeting its expectations and standards and hence achieving success? For success must be viewed contextually and in relation to some established criteria. There are those who view the typical public school as far too preoccupied with rigid conformity, force-feeding of meaningless curriculum, non-creativity, and sterile academics. Thus, promoting success with the disturbed child involves imposing these aspects of the public school upon him. Why not alter the system into which we are mainstreaming the child rather than perpetuating its imperfections and making the child conform? While this is a logical and penetrating question, I honestly do not believe it is realistic to dwell on while state education codes are rapidly moving toward facilitating mainstreaming and the process is actually under way. I believe the issue it raises, namely promoting better education for *all* children, can be dealt with while we are actually mainstreaming exceptional children into regular classrooms. That is, the process of mainstreaming with its emphasis on individualized instruction and guarantee of success may well result in regular class programs becoming better class programs for all children. What I am proposing is that we mainstream the exceptional child into the regular class program and concentrate on orchestrating his success at the very time we move toward helping regular classroom teachers broaden their ranges of tolerance for behavioral and academic differences so that all children are better served. There is no question in my mind that the mainstreaming phenomenon has the potential to greatly alter the American public school as special education merges with regular education, and better education for all children becomes our primary concern. I am sure that this approach to the issue of changing the system rather than changing the child to succeed within it will not be satisfactory to all. But I choose to pursue an action-oriented approach dealing with the reality of the here and now and strongly believe we can mainstream the child and alter the mainstream concurrently.

Back to the orchestration of success. It seems to me that we need to focus on the three variables that are critical for both individualized instruction and the guarantee of success—curriculum, conditions, and consequences. While I have discussed these variables elsewhere at length (Hewett 1974) in relation to special education, they warrant another look within the context of mainstreaming. The cornerstone of guaranteeing success may well be curriculum or the tasks we assign the child in the classroom. Closely related are the conditions under which we assign the task—when we ask him to work, where he works, how long we expect him to work, how much we expect him to do, and how well we expect him to function in order to meet our expectations. Finally, consequences or reinforcement are important because there must be something in it for the child which is positive in order to enlist his active participation as a learner in the classroom. These variables are derived from principles associated with operant methodology yet are described and defined for teacher consumption rather than theoretical referencing.

The behavior modification strategy which emerged in special education in the 1960s is concerned with engineering success for exceptional learners through the pinpointing of target behaviors to be taught, the recording of the child's responses, the setting of various contingencies associated with the delivery of positive reinforcement, and constant evaluation of the child's progress in order to make programmatic changes. The engineered classroom design (Hewett 1968) reflected the behavior modification strategy but involved a pragmatic educational framework that did not hold to precise targetting, response measurement, or evaluation. In many ways it might better have been called "the orchestrated classroom," conceived to accomplish the orchestration of success. And in many ways it may be advantageous to approach the regular educator in the 1970s who is involved with mainstreaming with the concept of "orchestrating" rather than "engineering" the child's success in the classroom. Over the years, I have been troubled by the communication breakdown that often occurred between humanistic, child-oriented educators and proponents of behavior modification methodology. As stated earlier there is no quarrel with individualizing instruction or guaranteeing success—these are components of good teaching for all children. But the semantic distortions often associated with "pinpointing target behavior" rather than "individualizing curriculum" and "reinforcing adaptive behavior" rather than "guaranteeing success" often lead to misunderstanding and rejection of many of the useful and effective aspects of behavior modification.

I believe the first step in the orchestrating of success involves refocus and re-emphasis on the curriculum variable. Behavior modifiers of the 1960s may have been too concerned with the mechanics of response rate measurement and reinforcement and not concerned enough with the nature of curriculum tasks assigned the child. A task selected for being what the child needs, what he is ready to do, and what he can be successful doing may implicitly involve appropriate conditions and rewarding consequences. That is the ideal Skinner discusses in the excerpt above. Thus, curriculum may inherently provide reinforcement for the child. As disturbed children are mainstreamed, assignment of such curriculum tasks in the regular classroom will be central to the orchestration of success.

In selecting such tasks we are going to have to be more creative and imaginative than most regular teachers usually find it necessary to be with their regular students, particularly in the upper elementary and secondary levels. However, "not finding it necessary to be creative and imaginative" may be the equivalent of "getting by with most of the students" rather than offering a truly stimulating and exciting learning environment. I have always been intrigued with the excitement for learning seen among kindergarteners, particularly when a resourceful and imaginative teacher works with them. It seems we dim this excitement quite quickly in the early grades and drudgery and boredom take its place. One of the aspects of kindergarten curriculum that accounts for its reinforcing properties is that just completing a task is fun since qualitative judgments of grading, accuracy, and comparisons with others' work are often minimized at this level. Another aspect is that emphasis in the curriculum is often on multisensory stimulation and movement. Looking, listening, touching, tasting, and moving are powerful reinforcers for insuring the child's active participation. Of course, social approval is well on its way to being a major reinforcement in the school at this level. The problem here is that with the disturbed child it may be of uncertain or even negative value after a grade or two of failure, frustration, and criticism.

In the elementary grades and even at the secondary level, I would like to see curricular options involving reinforcement on the task completion and multisensory level made available for the mainstreamed child (who knows how many other non-classified children might also profit!). The use of an order center where attention-response and order activities such as puzzles, pegboard designs, and sorting and matching activities are provided has been effective in the regular classroom. On the secondary level, I recall the teacher with a portable order center which he used as a non-academic alternative with students who "blew-up" or who had limited attention spans during scheduled activities. The center consisted of a muffin tin with assorted nuts and bolts all mixed together in the cups. The task assigned the child was to sort the nuts and bolts by size and to place like sizes in the same cup. I was impressed how this task given in a regular classroom with eighth grade students was accepted and enjoyed by all and how integral a part it was in the orchestration of success for particular students. I am not talking about "fun and games" in place of grade-level curriculum but about an extension of tasks available in the regular classroom, probably on a part-time and temporary basis, for children who are difficult to maintain as successful learners. Mainstreaming requires a broad definition of exactly what constitutes classroom curriculum. With only an academic set we are certain to fall short of our goal of making the integration of a disturbed child in a regular classroom a successful experience.

I had the opportunity to visit a residential program for disturbed children in another state. The program included a full-time school with three learning centers—academic, arts and crafts, and a movement lab. Children were free to choose where they wished to spend their time, and as might be expected, the academic center was often least preferred. In an attempt to deal with this problem, the staff decided to decentralize the academic work area and build reading and language arts tasks into the arts and crafts center and arithmetic tasks into the movement lab. Children would write about projects they were involved in, and undertake arithmetic problems related to physical education activities. Here is an example of creative curriculum at work, and while not directly applicable to the regular classroom, such embedding of academic lessons in social studies projects or arts and crafts activities might well prove useful in the orchestration of success.

In addition to viewing curriculum as embedding reinforcement, it may be useful to conceptualize reinforcement as creating curriculum for the regular classroom teacher involved in mainstreaming. For opportunities exist constantly throughout the class day for reinforcing certain desired behaviors and in the process creating a curriculum area right on the spot. It works something like this. The teacher sees Johnny raising his hand for assistance and says, "I see your hand, Johnny, and I appreciate your letting me know you need help. I'll be right with you." Johnny usually does not raise his hand but calls out in a loud voice. The curriculum area of "hand raising" simply has not been mastered by him. The teacher, by reinforcing his hand raising, is creating the curriculum area on the spot and teaching Johnny that this is an important behavior for success in the classroom. The centralist critics of mainstreaming (change the school, not the child) will undoutedly react negatively to this example. Why emphasize "hand raising"? Why suppress Johnny? Classrooms in which children must raise their hands are archaic! As a peripheralist (aid the child in adapting to the system and gradually work to better the system from within), I will defend the example and stand ready to give additional examples of curriculum related to "turn waiting," "seat sitting," "property respecting," "direction following," and "getting along with others." The point is that the regular teacher must realize that mainstreamed, disturbed children are often not ready to be successful in the regular classroom. If mainstreaming is to work and we are to lessen our reliance on self-contained programs to develop such readiness, the teacher must help get the child ready to be in the classroom while he is actually there. Curriculum with built-in reinforcement and reinforcement alerting the child to curriculum tasks important for success constitute approaches toward developing such readiness. In addition to social approval as a reinforcer, check mark systems or other acknowledgments may add vividness and be useful for selected mainstreamed children.

Continuing with a look at creative and imaginative curriculum and mainstreaming, let us consider other possibilities. Mercer (1971) found that mildly retarded children who had a friend in a regular classroom were less likely to be referred out for special class placement than their friendless counterparts. One curriculum area which may be important to focus on in mainstreaming is "promoting a friendship" through peer tutoring and assignment of pairs of children to various projects or classroom duties, although this will necessitate careful "sizing up" of all children. The concept of a "big brother" or "big sister" also may be appropriate to explore in certain situations. This suggestion relates to a broader concern, namely capitalizing on every opportunity for appropriate behavioral and language modeling to aid the disturbed child. One of the real problems associated with self-contained class placement for disturbed children is that they are more often surrounded by models of what not to do rather than what to do. Mainstreaming may prove valuable in altering this situation by exposing the child to children who have been more adequately socialized and who are successful students. The same concern exists with the retarded child. How much of the difficulty retarded children experience sizing up social situations appropriately and acting independently is actually due to limited experience and modeling rather than retardation *per se*? Again, self-contained placement provides little opportunity for appropriate modeling. In an effort to capitalize on opportunities for promoting friendships and modeling, we may have to consider such opportunities the primary reason for integrating the disturbed child and not worry as much about whether the child can participate in scheduled activities. There are some who will react to this statement with, "Aha! Now he's let us know he views mainstreaming as a babysitting service!" I hope notions of readiness training, learning-competence acquisition, and building of socialization skills will overshadow such a simplistic reaction. I believe exposing the disturbed child to a normal classroom environment is a most respectable curriculum activity and that the specific task he undertakes may be of secondary importance. However, unless the regular teacher understands and accepts such broad statements of purpose associated with mainstreaming and continually focuses on the individual child in terms of what he needs to learn, is ready to learn, and can be successful learning, "babysitting" rather than "creative teaching" may be the more accurate description.

This brings up an important issue related to the special educator's role in mainstreaming. Whatever the new title—resource specialist, resource teacher, or special consultant—as special educators become increasingly involved with the orchestration of success in the regular classroom, emphasis must be placed on defining what it is the classroom really has to offer the child, what he is ready to profit from, and the specific times and activities during which learning and success are most likely to occur. Such concerns probably constitute the core concept of the orchestration of success.

In the Santa Monica Madison School Plan, determination of an exceptional child's mainstreaming potential is linked to his functioning level in four areas: (1) pre-academic functioning, (2) academic functioning, (3) the ability to work in various classroom settings or groupings, and (4) the susceptibility to incentives available in the classroom. While no formal diagnostic procedure is utilized, the special educator describes the child within each of these areas when introducing him to a regular classroom teacher. Thus, Mary is introduced as needing pre-academic emphasis in taking part orally in group discussion, needing particular help with reading comprehension, is able to work best in individual or small group settings, and as being very susceptible to social praise. Tom, on the other hand, has difficulty following directions, is at a first grade level in reading, needs an individual instructional setting, and is best reinforced by the giving of check marks since he becomes anxious when the teacher verbally praises him. With this information available, Mary and Tom may well be closer to experiencing something positive from integration into the regular classroom.

The mainstreaming phenomenon has arrived across the nation whether special or regular education is ready for it or not. Much study is going to be necessary to determine exactly how it can provide better education for disturbed children. This chapter has stressed the orchestration of success through creative conceptualization of curriculum as a major approach in optimizing mainstreaming.

REFERENCES

Hewett, F. M. *The Emotionally Disturbed Child in the Classroom.* Boston: Allyn & Bacon, 1968.

———, with S. Forness. *Education of Exceptional Learners.* Boston: Allyn & Bacon, 1974.

Mercer, J. "The Meaning of Mental Retardation." In *The Mentally Retarded Child and His Family,* edited by R. Koch and J. Dobson. New York: Brunner/Mazel, 1971.

Skinner, B. F. "Teaching: The Arrangement of Contingencies under which Something is Taught." In *The Improvement of Instruction,* edited by N. Haring and A. Hayden. Seattle: Special Child Publications, 1972.

7

Implications for Leadership Training

FRANK H. WOOD

P ROVIDING LEADERSHIP in the introduction or strengthening of mainstreaming as a special education programming option is an exercise
in personal diplomacy. The consultant, administrator, or teacher interested in promoting mainstreaming should have well in mind a comprehensive model of special education services and be alert to some
recurrent problems in introducing this option.

THE BASIC GOALS OF SPECIAL EDUCATION

We special educators cannot confine our attention to mainstreaming as a
single programming option because such a single alternative is insuffi-
ciently flexible to match the requirements of our basic goals. The rationale
for these goals will not be stated here in detail. However, they spring
from legislation, administrative regulations, and court decisions, as well
as ethical considerations and the findings of behavioral research.

A basic goal is the identification of *educationally* exceptional children. The special educator's concern is not necessarily with all children
who are handicapped as defined by medical parameters. As Rubin and
Balow (1971) have said, "Those in need of special education [should]
be identified behaviorally by their inability to make satisfactory progress
under regular education" (p. 293). The specific aspect of educational
exceptionality implied by this definition in the phrases "satisfactory
progress" and "regular education" will not be discussed here. Let us
assume that we are talking about disturbed/disturbing students in schools
as they are.

In providing such students with a more appropriate education, the special educator is guided by the principle of the "least restrictive" situation. That is to say, he will remove the educationally exceptional child from the "regular" school situation shared with his peers only if necessary for the child's education or because the child's behavior is *extremely* destructive of the learning environment of his peers. If placement in an alternative situation is necessary, the special educator will seek to remove the child from the regular situation for the shortest possible time and to the shortest possible distance—for example, to the part-time resource room rather than the full-day special class; the special program in the same building or community as the regular class rather than the residential school. In every case, the intention is to provide the educationally exceptional child with an *appropriate educational experience*— that experience which will be most efficacious for the development of his potential.

Dr. Edwin W. Martin, Deputy Commissioner of the Bureau of Education for the Handicapped, has a knack for pinpointing critical issues. In the November 1974 issue of *Exceptional Children,* he discusses the positive concern for the life experience of handicapped persons that has led to the efforts to design mainstream programs in accordance with the principles that have been mentioned. But, as he notes, we must always return to the first principles. Our goal is not to mainstream educationally exceptional children. Our goal is to provide them with an appropriate education, and mainstreaming is an option that will be the most appropriate for many but not all. But, to quote Martin, "We must also avoid those well-intentioned lies that ignore the weaknesses in a well-intentioned system, because we are afraid that exposure will hurt our cause. We should not allow our belief in the promises of mainstreaming to cause us to be silent if we see faults in its application. With the newly recognized rights of children to the education we offer, there must be an equal responsibility to see that those rights are truly fulfilled" (p. 153).

Leaders who are fundamentally committed to providing appropriate educational opportunities for disturbed/disturbing children must be willing to respond honestly to Martin's challenge.

A RANGE OF ALTERNATIVES

In the mid-fifties the problems faced by most large city special educators were different than they are now. At that time, many young people were simply excluded from school because of their disturbing behavior. Our first goal was to get behavior problem children back into the school-house. Now, in our efforts to operationalize the principle of appropriate education in the least restrictive situation, we are seeking to provide both more fully differentiated and individualized programs in the regular classroom and a range of alternative situations, progressively more restrictive in the sense of distance from the mainstream, but each appropriate for some disturbed/disturbing children. One way of looking at a range of alternatives is in terms of what Evelyn Deno (1970) has called a "cascade model." If by mainstreaming we mean providing special education to educationally exceptional children who are in regular classes for one-half or more of each school day, then the mainstream would include these levels of the cascade model. What are some salient issues in implementing mainstream programs?

ANTICIPATING PROBLEMS IN IMPLEMENTING MAINSTREAM PROGRAMS

Fred Hechinger, then education editor of *The New York Times,* made an interesting observation in his July 10, 1966, column reviewing the demise of New York's Higher Horizons Program for educationally disadvantaged students. He noted the very real success of Higher Horizons when it was originally instituted as a pilot program. Competent, highly motivated teachers volunteered for the program from all over New York City. This high-powered staff was provided with additional support funds from foundation grants. As a result, they had the benefit of support services and materials not available to other teachers. Student progress was gratifying. But, when an effort was made to generalize the program to other city schools, success was extremely limited. Funds were far less than had been available for the pilot program. Class sizes were larger. Support services were not available, etc., etc. Hechinger suggests that to generalize on a large scale from a successful pilot project requires more rather than less financial support. Without fully adequate resources, an exemplary program may continue to function for a short time if its personnel have an extraordinary commitment. When these human resources are exhausted, the program dies.

The history of the Higher Horizons Program is instructive as we think about providing leadership to mainstreaming efforts for disturbed and disturbing children. The fact that mainstreaming programs have been successful on a small scale or in some systems does not mean that they will not flop in others. There are a number of problems that we can anticipate as we plan to develop the mainstreaming option in other than pilot situations. By anticipating, we may avoid them or solve them when they arise.

1. We must be prepared to deal with defensive attitudes in both regular and special education administrators and teachers. The "disastrous inadequacy" of segregated special education classes has been widely discussed in recent years, although as Hammons (1972) has pointed out, the research basis for such statements is weak. However, one result has been to place special class teachers on the defensive. The promotion of mainstreaming has frequently been associated with criticism of the adequacy of the special class program rather than with stress on the need to provide a broadened range of appropriate alternatives in instruction for mildly and moderately disabled learners. The implication is that special class teachers should "confess their sins," convert to resource teachers, and join their critics in promoting mainstreaming. Not all those new converts are with us.

In the same way that special class teachers have been made defensive by attacks on the efficacy of the special class that have frequently accompanied increased stress on mainstreaming, regular class teachers have been sensitive to the charge that they are seeking to dump disturbing children out of the mainstream without considering their individual rights or needs. Those of us who are committed to the encouragement of mainstreaming may decry such attitude, but we will be wise if we include ways of dealing with them as part of our mainstreaming strategy. Teachers are not without means of defense that can wreck our programs. Even committed administrators will not press on in the face of too much teacher resistance.

For example, the defensiveness of regular classroom teachers can be seen in clauses specifically excluding disturbed/disturbing children in some contracts submitted by teacher organizations in districts where collective bargaining occurs. Birch (1974) notes that teacher consent for pupil placement is required by contract in the Tucson Public School, although he states that no grievances have yet been filed under this provision of the contract.

How do we deal constructively with this defensiveness? First, we should watch what we say. Why arouse anxiety unnecessarily by placing blame or calling mainstreaming "new"? Mainstreaming is not new. Regular classroom teachers need not be frightened of having educationally exceptional children in their classes for they have many of them in their classes all along. Furthermore, mainstreaming is not so much a refusal of special educators to continue to serve certain exceptional learners as it is an expression of confidence in the ability of regular classroom teachers to provide these children with a more appropriate education than they can receive in special situations if given appropriate support.

If we note that the administrators and teachers with whom we are dealing in this situation are genuinely disturbed themselves, we can better plan how to proceed. We are asking them to make changes in their professional roles. We are asking them to take some difficult steps in areas where we can provide no sure answers. This is bound to produce stress. Rather than attempting to force mainstreaming on them in an arrogant, authoritarian manner or presenting a super sales pitch, we might employ some of the techniques that we have used effectively with disturbed children in the past. Remember the basic concept of the life space interview: Listen first to what the disturbed/disturbing person has to say about what is happening. Then proceed to share and discuss a different perception of reality, your own or that of others, making it clear that it is a person rather than a supernatural being speaking.

Incidentally, defensiveness is not a unique characteristic of *others*. What about ourselves? Special education "leaders" may not be prepared to face the implications of giving up categorical labels that comfortably support the separate educational stream. Where will we take our stand if caught in a cost squeeze?

The willingness of white liberal professionals to demand equal employment opportunities in the building trades was greater than their support for affirmative action as applied to positions in their own departments. Special educators, this writer included, have sometimes opposed the use of limited categorical funds to support mainstreaming activities because we felt greater priority for their use should be given to programs for poorly served or unserved severely handicapped children such as those showing autistic-type behavior. Real world choices come hard.

At the same time, we should avoid forcing the mainstreaming notion even if it is in our power to do so. The *strongest* support for the concept of mainstreaming at present is rational: legal and ethical. Research evidence in my opinion is neither stronger nor weaker than the evidence for and against the efficacy of the special class. Some selected mainstreaming programs are highly successful. Others have limited impact (see Warfield 1974). The fact that the problem may be in the teacher rather than the student, the disturbed rather than the disturbing, does not change the impact on that student. The interest on *our* commitment to mainstream *should not be paid by children* already bruised in classroom conflicts. We can rationalize these actions by bad-mouthing regular educators for their supposed inattention to the special needs of educationally exceptional children, but where are we if they show us we are focusing on the past and begin to demonstrate the leadership we have said they would not take? Will we remove our blinders, drop *our* special status, and develop a broad concern for all children? There is no easy answer here. This writer likes what Hewett (1974) says about living with "dissonance" as one test of the realism of our theoretical posture *vis-à-vis* the "real world." Dealing with issues is harder when they get closer to home.

2. In implementing mainstreaming programs, we need to explore possibilities for synchronizing the perceptions of teachers and administrators of the behavior of disturbed/disturbing pupils. The first step is to be sure everyone is talking about the same thing: Group monologs are frequent when disturbing behavior is the topic. At the University of Minnesota, several of us have been exploring methods for clarifying perceptions of the behavior of children with whom teachers find themselves in conflict (Wood and Brazil 1974; Brazil and Wood 1974; Burns 1974). We treat the conflict, the distress felt by both teacher and pupil, as real. Our approach is to ask if we may observe the pupil so as to develop a more complete picture of the disturbing behavior. We do not challenge directly the authority of the teacher to define and enforce norms for classroom behavior. However, we suggest that any person dealing with a large group of pupils will naturally have found it difficult to observe all of the behavior of a pupil who seems to be a problem. Our observation procedure stresses the recording of instances of positive as well as negative interaction between the observed pupil and classroom peers. We observe a randomly selected group of same sex peers at the same time we observe the target pupil. We can then sit down immediately with the teacher to discuss what we have observed of the pupil's behavior. We find that teachers frequently state that they have been made aware anew of the positive behavior of pupils who had been viewed only as disturbers. We also get spontaneous requests for help that sanction a discussion of the teacher's behavior: "What can I do?" Graubard (1969) reported a similar change in the perception of behavior reported spontaneously by acting-out pupils after they observed their acting-out peer group through a one-way screen.

Looking for positive behavior as well as disturbing behavior has proved to be very helpful. We have found, somewhat to our surprise

(Brazil and Wood 1974) that pupils referred as severe acting-out behavior problems showed more *positive* interactions with their peers than did the comparison group of nonreferred pupils. Higher frequency of occurrence of negative behavior was anticipated; higher frequency of positive behavior was contrary to predictions and may have been sample specific. But it was there, and teachers agreed it was there when it was pointed out. We have found more recently that brief instruction in the use of this observation procedure that stressed looking for positive as well as negative behaviors in problem pupils caused a significant difference in the noting of positive behaviors in a group of teachers who had been so instructed as compared to a non-instructed contrast group (Burns 1974).

An example may be helpful. A teacher asked that a girl in her sixth grade class be removed immediately. The school psychologist who received the referral asked for and received permission to observe Mary in the classroom as part of planning for an appropriate placement. The behavior pattern that emerged in the observation record was one of much activity, most of it summarizable in a general category we have come to call "positive but inappropriate" rather than appearing to be negative in intent. "Positive but inappropriate" behavior is behavior of apparently positive intent that comes out at the "wrong" time. The teacher asks John what time it is. Bill, who is being observed, blurts out, "Oh, teacher! It's fifteen after ten." Bill's verbalization falls into our "positive but inappropriate" category.

When Mary, her teacher, and the psychologist sat down to discuss her behavior, Mary's eyes quickly filled with tears. "I was afraid you didn't like me," she wept. "And I'm trying so hard to be good." This classroom problem situation was not solved by the simultaneous insights Mary and her teacher had about how Mary's best efforts to please were leading her to disturb her teacher even more, but an important first step was taken. Agreement was reached on what the problem was, and plans were made to work on it in the classroom through helping Mary experiment with judgments of "when" to try to please, while at the same time providing her with more frequent opportunities for the physical activity she needed.

Note that teachers are not asked to forget about the behavior that they find disturbing. Rather, they are encouraged to view it in a broader context when planning interventions. This subtle change in viewpoint counteracts the tendency to screen out positive behaviors that frequently precede the scapegoating of a victim. Stated more positively, it provides the basis for hope that something more positive can be done. Tensions ease a bit while we discuss alternative solutions, including remaining in the mainstream.

3. We must provide the resources necessary to support a mainstreaming program. Some advocates of mainstreaming have suggested that it will be cheaper than present special educational programming. It has been suggested that money will be saved in terms of a need for smaller numbers of special education personnel and in transportation costs. This is unwise. Viewed in the perspective of a total special education program developed along the lines of the cascade model, a program that will serve *all* educationally exceptional children appropriately, rather than just a program that channels exceptional learners back into regular classrooms, will require more funding than is provided in most school districts at the present time.

To further complicate matters, state aid funds or even local funds available to support exceptional learners in special classes may not be available to support those same students if they are served in the regular class. The advocate of mainstreaming should anticipate such difficulties and initiate remedies. For example, legislation can provide special education funds to support personnel on the basis of funding estimates projected relative to percentages of school enrollment. Funds to support services for 4–5 percent of the total school population estimated to be *severely* handicapped educationally can be joined to funds to support an additional 6–7 percent less severely handicapped who are served through increased accommodation by the mainstream. Such procedures supply services through a broad range of professional roles without labeling children as is done by "per pupil" patterns of reimbursement. Special educators should seek to take the initiative on such matters so that changes in policy and regulation can precede rather than follow programming interventions.

As has already been argued with reference to the Higher Horizons Program, general implementation of any new program should be budgeted with more money rather than less. For example, a successful mainstreaming effort will often require some reduction of class size. One of the most unfortunate myths that we have taught to the past two generations of regular classroom teachers is the belief that it is possible to "individualize" instruction in classes of any size. Most teachers have not been adequately taught how to individualize instruction effectively in classes of *any* size. Educationally exceptional pupils in regular classrooms are frequently poorly taught because there is not enough instructional time to go around, given the methods used by the teacher. Smaller class size, appropriate materials, teacher aides—these are a partial list of the kinds of resources that must be used to back up a mainstreaming effort. This suggests a need for special education's support of increased funding for regular education programs.

4. We must provide new skills for both special and regular educators to support the mainstreaming operation. Providing additional resources, lowering class size, providing additional materials, classroom aides, and supportive personnel is not enough. Teachers do not automatically make use of additional resources effectively. This was pointed out by David Fox in his discussion of the disappointing results of the More Effective Schools Project in New York City (1968). While some of the defenders of the More Effective Schools Program stressed weaknesses in the research design, the weaknesses were no more exceptional than those typical in evaluation studies. Also, more persuasive explanations could be offered. Fox pointed out that the teacher inservice training aspect of the plan was one part that had never been fully implemented. He suggested that had teachers been taught better how to use the resources provided, his finding that teacher behavior in classes of twenty was not different from teacher behavior in classes of thirty might well have been different. Regardless of the merits in that particular controversy, Fox's point is instructive.

We must provide more than supportive resources if mainstreaming is to succeed. *We must also provide instruction to teachers on how to use those resources.*

5. Teachers are aware that they need to have knowledge and skills they do not now have (Birch 1974; McCauley and Deno 1975). But where does the acquisition of such knowledge and skills fit in their list of priorities? Other issues such as racial conflict or political pressure from educational reactionaries can drain off the attention and energy of school personnel who must implement the new programs. *Can we motivate regular and special class personnel to acquire the skills that we know they must have if mainstreaming is to be successful?* This will be the real test of our leadership, just as arousing and using the motivation of our pupils has always been the teacher's greatest instructional problem. Whatever we have learned about motivation must be applied to teachers if we expect to be successful. We have begun with scolding. We are proceeding to ask them to accept responsibility for the education of exceptional pupils under conditions that make that responsibility appear to be an extra burden. If in addition to accepting that "extra burden," we also expect them to undergo additional special training, we must provide some sort of positive inducements for their cooperation if we are to have a chance of success with any but the most idealistic. This means re-

leased time for training and perhaps for supportive counseling. If training is carried on outside of the school day, it must be on a voluntary basis and with the provision of appropriate compensation. We plan for "motivating" children to learn; we must plan for motivating their teachers.

Lest it be thought that concern with financial or other compensation for school personnel receiving training is always altruistic, the would-be mainstreamer is reminded to check early to determine if such matters are regulated by contract or school board policy. In many districts, times for training and rates of compensation are specified in detail.

6. What role will parents and pupils have in decisions about mainstreaming? Looking at the mainstreaming movement, one sometimes has the feeling that while it is strongly supported by some parents, it is something laid on others by professionals. There is little evidence that the wishes of individual pupils or parents are consulted in the implementation of this program option. Mainstreaming is better for them because we special education leaders say so; no questions, please. We are the major definers of what is satisfactory or unsatisfactory progress.

The issue is a complex one. In the case of pupils, Jones (1974) has noted the rejection of special classes and negative labels by special class pupils. But in follow-up studies, he reports relatively more positive attitudes toward school on the part of children in special classes than those in regular classes. Extrapolating from such group data causes us to assume that individual special class students may well be pleased to be where they are. Is our professional opinion that their special class placement is less appropriate and their progress unsatisfactory to be acted on without discussion, or will their attitudes and those of their parents be consulted before they are mainstreamed? They should be, and mainstreaming should be presented to them as one option in alternative educational programming. We have just begun to recognize the right of children and their parents to choose among a variety of educational options such as open schools, traditional schools, continuous progress schools, free schools. We can certainly urge our viewpoint, but the right to a choice about what happens to one's life should not be lost when a pupil is identified as educationally exceptional.

I have talked personally with possessors of high school diplomas who could not read after having been "mainstreamed" for all of their educational careers. They felt they had been deprived of a chance to choose. Recent court cases, such as the Peter Doe case in California, suggest that court decisions will soon cause us to give attention to parent and pupil satisfaction with educational programming (Abel 1974).

Certainly a minimal defense against educational malpractice would seem to require special educators to provide evidence of informed consent to the special education alternative implemented. Gallagher (1972) and Wood (1973) have focused attention on this aspect of intervention planning and have presented legally sanctioned and less formal alternative models.

CONCLUSIONS

This brings us back to Martin's comment. The burden is on those of us taking leadership in the mainstreaming movement to provide evidence that this new stress in programming leads to more appropriate education for disturbed and disturbing pupils. Criticism of alternative programming is not proof of the greater efficacy of the "new model" we propose. While we know we can demonstrate that mainstreaming has worked well in certain classrooms and for certain students, we must prepare ourselves to report honestly to parents and pupils about its effectiveness in their particular cases. We must also demand accountability for placement decisions that remove the educationally exceptional to special situations.

Our professional responsibility is not to sell mainstreaming. Our responsibility is to provide to educationally exceptional children, who are disturbed or disturbing, an educational program that will enable them to develop their unique potential for the benefit of themselves and the rest of us, their fellow citizens. If we are provided with the necessary resources, and if we use our pooled knowledge and skill, we will reach that goal while helping the great majority of the educationally exceptional to swim strongly in the mainstream.

REFERENCES

Abel, D. "Can a Student Sue the Schools for Educational Malpractice? Case of *Peter Doe* v. *San Francisco Unified School District.*" *Harvard Educational Review* 44 (1974): 416–36.

Birch, J. W. *Mainstreaming Educable Mentally Retarded Children in Regular Classes.* Reston, Va.: Council for Exceptional Children, 1974.

Brazil, N. R., and Wood, F. H. "Broadening Our Perspective on the Behavior of Children Referred for Special Class Placement as Behavior Problems." Mimeo. 1974.

Burns, H. M. "The Effect of the Use of Systematic Behavior Observation Procedures on the Perception of Severe Behavior Problem Children by Teachers." Unpublished doctoral dissertation. Minneapolis: University of Minnesota, 1974.

Deno, E. "Special Education as Developmental Capital." *Exceptional Children* 37 (1970): 229–37.

Fox, D. J. P.C.: "Evaluating the 'More Effective Schools.'" *Phi Delta Kappan* 49 (1968): 593–97.

Gallagher, J. J. "The Special Education Contract for Mildly Handicapped Children." *Exceptional Children* 38 (1972): 527–35.

Graubard, P. S. "Utilizing the Group in Teaching Disturbed Delinquents to Learn." *Exceptional Children* 36 (1969): 267–72.

Hammons, G. W. "Educating the Mildly Retarded: A Review." *Exceptional Children* 38 (1972): 565–70.

Hewett, F. M., with Forness, S. R. *Education of Exceptional Learners.* Boston: Allyn & Bacon, 1974.

Jones, R. L. "Student Views of Special Placement and Their Own Special Classes: A Clarification." *Exceptional Children* 41 (1974): 22–29.

Martin, E. W. "Some Thoughts on Mainstreaming." *Exceptional Children* 41 (1974): 150–53.

McCauley, R. W., and Deno, S. L. "Resource Teacher Perceptions of Difficulties Confronted in a First-Year Resource Program." *CCBD Newsletter* 12 (1975): 7–10.

Rubin, R., and Balow, B. E. "Learning and Behavior Disorders: A Longitudinal Study." *Exceptional Children* 38 (1971): 292–99.

Warfield, G. J., ed. *Mainstream Currents: 1968–1974.* Reston, Va.: Council for Exceptional Children, 1974.

Wood, F. H. "Negotiation and Justification: An Intervention Model." *Exceptional Children* 40 (1973): 185–90.

——, and Brazil, N. R. "Looking for the Good and the Bad in 'Problem' Children." Mimeo. 1974.

8

Implications for Teacher Preparation

ALBERT H. FINK

HOW MANY MUST HAVE WINCED as the echoes of Dunn's immortal words were heard as a call to arms against those efforts to rehabilitate the emotionally disturbed who stood outside the portals of the regular classroom. It was difficult to accept that the emergent structure was alien, that regularized educational environments possessed the magical incantations necessary for the personal transformation of the difficult, the disturbed or merely disturbing, or the maladjusted. How many must have wondered at the facility with which theoretical tides turned, at the suddenness with which forces were marshaled to create the conditions for mass migrations of problem youngsters into the muddied streams of the everyday. How many teachers and parents must have asked how it could be imperatively, or so it seemed, desirable to believe what was, yesterday, so clearly undesirable. Was history to be rewritten, the past ignored, or conveniently forgotten?

Such historical data that is available suggests that, in the modern era, education's part in society's response to the behaviorally disordered (to make use of yet another descriptor) was one which at first deferred to the primacy of others (Fink and Glass 1973). This understandable posture, understandable in view of the pressures of large numbers of difficult-to-deal with children combined with the *noblesse oblige* of the helping professions, was soon weakened as a result of the clear inadequacy of the attempted solution and of theories suggesting new roles for the public school system in the direct treatment process (Bower and Hollister 1967). As the public school system's direct response to the needs of the behaviorally disordered evolved, diverse program responses were provided with the "special class" as an important and visible element

101

(Morse, Cutler, and Fink 1964). While theoretical orientations varied widely, the special class, as a service vehicle, represented a significant part of the treatment process and was viewed as one link in a relatively fluid system for the provision of needed services to the disturbed child. It might be appropriate to note that a unique characteristic of special classes for the emotionally disturbed, when compared to earlier classes for the retarded, was the assumption that placement was not by definition, and of necessity, permanent. Disturbed children could be cured and thus be returned to regular classes; and this became an objective of the special class. For the retarded child, the "truly retarded," could such hopes be held? For the latter, special classes could only mean permanently separate paths.

Most significant in the development of the public school's role in the treatment for the emotionally disturbed were the conceptual developments alluded to earlier which have tended to place squarely in the hands of suitably trained professional educators the primary responsibility and influence necessary for effecting change (Fink 1972; Long, Morse, and Newman 1971). This is not to say that the traditional helping professions do not have a vital role to play; it is merely that the formal educative process contains within it the stuff of treatment, and the responsible educator, the educator trained in the science and art of teaching the emotionally handicapped, is the crucial person in the crucial arena. For the school system and the other institutions engaged in providing services, some rearrangement of relationships and responsibilities took place. A less unequal balance, the cynic might say, was set.

Credence has been given to the potential impact of the educator, whether in the public school directly or within hospital/clinic/residential center/school programs, by the federal government. Funding patterns initiated by the Bureau for the Education of the Handicapped (BEH) have directly or indirectly resulted in special education teacher training programs in some two hundred colleges and universities. These continue to place considerable emphasis on the training of teachers to work with the behaviorally disordered (Fink, Glass, and Guskin 1975). Broad-based professional support for the role of the specially trained teacher and the special education system in the treatment of the behaviorally disordered also came through the imprimatur of the Report of the Joint Commission on Mental Health of Children (1970).

It is against this backdrop that current concerns and issues regarding the formal school system and its part in the rehabilitative process must be understood. Adequate responsiveness to the behaviorally disordered by the public school network will require clarity of concepts about the nature of the phenomenon and the precise responsibilities of all those involved, directly or indirectly, in the process. Above all, slogans adopted to rally support for this or that approach demand careful analysis. For reasons which lie beyond the scope of this chapter, special educators appear willing to move with alacrity when confronted with the new or the apparently new. A term such as "mainstreaming" has immediate seductiveness; what its meaning is, and its possible impact upon the results of many years of hard, dedicated work on behalf of the emotionally disturbed needs more than superficial inquiry. The special concern of this chapter then is the challenge directed at teacher education by that aspect of mainstreaming which embraces the emotionally disturbed.

ASSUMPTIONS OF THE MAINSTREAMING MOVEMENT

The thrust of the mainstreaming movement, motivated by Dunn's 1968 critique, has aimed at providing handicapped children with educational services that depend less heavily than in the past upon special self-contained classes, combined with a greater utilization of the regular classroom. The former placements have been viewed as inadequate for many handicapped children and have resulted in major calls for reappraisal of educational programming for the mildly and/or moderately handicapped. The general debates which have ensued (Reynolds and Davis 1971; Birch 1974; Chaffin 1974; Deno, undated) describe numerous prescriptive alternatives to the classic "special education model" and will not be reviewed. It will be necessary to consider the major assumptions of mainstreaming, however, and to consider their importance for the education of the emotionally disturbed. It is necessary to do this if for no other reason than mainstreaming, although not originally intended for the emotionally disturbed, is being applied to that population with increasing frequency. No discriminations, or so it seems to many, are being made between the disturbed and the mildly retarded in terms of the application of the concept. Exceptional children are far from being a homogeneous group, however, and some distinctions may be in order.

    1. A basic assumption is that special educational practice results in unnecessary exclusion of many children from the fundamental social-psychological community of the school. This exclusion has, it is believed,

numerous negative effects which are related primarily to academic achievement and self-valuing. Many handicapped children thus would be better off if returned to the regular classroom and provided with supportive services focusing on individual needs.

2. A second major assumption is that a different set of balances will exist between special educators and regular educators. Fink and Glass (1973), as well as others, have described this as an active-advocacy" role for special education as opposed to a "reactive-advocacy," in which there is "a greater willingness . . . to tackle the broader and more intensive issues of the larger educational process" (p. 144).

3. A third assumption, which may at first appear paradoxical, is that there will be increasing concern for services for difficult children as opposed to settings in which they might be provided. Mainstreaming implies meeting needs optimally, and is not necessarily a focus upon the formal setting in which services are provided.

Clearly the mainstreaming movement implies that there is value in the everyday school structure for many children who are not now there. As interpreted by many, mainstreaming means the movement of virtually *all* children who are in specialized programs into regular classrooms. Whether or not a radical or moderate view gains the ascendancy, it is clear that many more disturbed children will be expected to function successfully in more regularized settings. For this to have any hope for success, however, many changes in school practice will have to occur. If they do not, we shall have returned to an earlier, less satisfactory phase of educational practice, in which the vast majority of others requiring assistance were lost in the ineptness of everyday practice.

It is important to stress that the typical regular school practices of the historical present offer little cause for optimism about the systems' potential for educating the behaviorally disordered even with sophisticated support. The typical regular classroom is not noted for its flexibility in accommodating child variance and, as noted previously, has teamed with special education to move problem children out of the mainstream. Pressures for implementing this exclusion process have a number of specific reasons:

1. Inability or unwillingness to tolerate deviant behavior.
2. Lack of skills in behavioral management.
3. Failure to understand the fullest purpose of education.
4. Genuine belief in the values of exclusion.
5. Parental insistence upon "special help."
6. Perceptions of the exclusivity of the needs of normal children.

To provide for a reversal of this process, which will have ultimate meaning for children, important changes in practice must occur. Without these changes, mainstreaming will be an empty term indeed.

THE ADVANTAGES OF SPECIAL EDUCATION
FOR THE BEHAVIORALLY DISORDERED

For mainstreaming to be effective, it will be necessary to examine not only the advantages which are expected to accrue naturally from regular class placement, but also to give specific attention to the advantages of the special educational process which one might wish to retain. The establishment of new functional relationships between regular and special education ought not to obscure the validity of benefits which accrue to the behaviorally disordered through special class placements. While confession of one's sins is doubtless beneficial, there is something to be said for recognition of one's acts of grace.

In the view of this writer, there have been important benefits to the behaviorally disordered through participation in special educational programs; benefits which are often obscured by the rhetoric of the day. Let us call these benefits "The Three R's of Special Education": (1) respite, (2) repair, (3) renewal.

While there are many approaches to the definition of disturbed behavior, one typical definition, which most of us might agree to, is that it reflects the operation of a network of tension, stress, and discomfort which has as its focal point the child. The "problem child" in the regular classroom, more often than not, has a "cumulative record" of such states and has little opportunity for constructive relief from the situation in which he finds himself. For many children the special class provides needed *respite*. One is reminded of the value attributed to "retreats," so common among religious orders, for those under stress. Respite is not avoidance, however, and is linked to the second of the "Three R's of Special Education," *repair*. The emotionally disturbed child finds himself, in the first place, under great and continuing strain. The anxiety created by the situation mitigates against the development of new skills— in the typical regular classroom. Special class placement aids in the acquisition of new behaviors then, by first providing respite, and by offering well-tailored new skills in the management of one's self and the world one is in (repair). The well-defined special class will generate further experiences which, when combined with changes brought about both by respite and repair, will allow for the *renewal* of the whole person. This admittedly idealized and overlapping set of objectives of the special class for the emotionally disturbed is its higher purpose and one which is carried out in many programs across the country. The importance of the "Three R's" should not be lost in mainstreaming models.

To recapitulate: the failure of many children to succeed within regularized educational programs provided the impetus for the development of the special educational system. This network offered services to a wide variety of exceptional children. Many mildly and moderately handicapped children placed in special classes for the educable mentally retarded were viewed as misplaced; recommendations to move these children back to regular classes laid the groundwork for the mainstreaming movement which, in varying degrees, has urged the "decertification" of large numbers of exceptional children, including the behaviorally disordered. For this movement to succeed, the original starting point for these children cannot be as it was. The changes required must acknowledge the advantages which have been available within special settings and provide for them within the operational statement that reflects mainstreaming.

TEACHER PREPARATION—WHAT?

Whatever model of mainstreaming is adopted for the behaviorally disordered, it is clear that the regular classroom teacher will have greater accountability than at present for successful outcomes. While supportive specialists (instructional specialists, resource consultants, special class teachers) all continue to be highlighted in the mainstreaming movement, a large part of its success will depend on regular classroom teachers who have different skills mixes than presently held. As with service delivery systems to children, teacher preparation has seen a "clear split" between special education and regular education. It would not be an exaggeration to say that typically a teacher who plans to work with exceptional children follows a training path, in the professional areas at least, that would only by accident resemble that taken by a future elementary teacher. While valid arguments occasionally surface on the question of "how special is special education?" there can be no denying that a considerable body of knowledge about exceptional children and methods for working with them has developed over the past twenty years. This is as true for the behaviorally disordered as it is for other exceptionalities. Teachers who teach the behaviorally disordered have much to draw from what is distinctive and effective, and this methodology is not, one might observe, merely techniques of "behavioral control," though these are important. So one might reasonably expect special education trainers to cast a possessive eye over certain of the training content for regular teachers.

What changes are needed in regular education training? As pointed out earlier, regular teachers, at the very least, must have some new behavioral possibilities in their repertoire. Providing regular classroom teachers with additional skills will raise the threshold of tolerance for the behaviorally disordered, raise the competence of teachers to cope; it would reduce the referral flow of targeted children, on the one hand, and increase the "successibility" of problem children on the other. These are perhaps self-evident points. Yet practice does not always reflect the axiomatic.

Improving the skills of regular classroom teachers is important for another reason. The laudable emphasis upon the preparation of specially trained teachers has created a class of well-trained, sophisticated professionals—an elite—who possess jargon, skills, and knowledge not shared by those they are now especially asked to work with most closely. Useful involvement by regular teachers thus demands greater understanding and skill in specialized processes. As pointed out earlier, the self-perceived inadequacy, based on accurate reality testing of regular teachers to deal with different and/or difficult behaviors, serves as a powerful stimulus for the referral (or rejection) of children displaying these behaviors to the support systems within and without the school system. While academic failure is a strong motive for referral, there is widespread documentation to attest that the critical problems of teachers are those of management and control, that these are, as a class, the single most pressing issue for teachers, regular and special alike (Hewett and Blake 1973; Morse, Cutler, and Fink 1964). Individual and group management skills then are the most critically needed skills for regular classroom teachers if a more successful utilization of the regular classroom is to be accomplished. The "what?" of teacher preparation thus means, to a very considerable degree, a focus upon skill development.

But like so many other of the jargon phrases, "individual and group management skills" means different things to different people—one set of activities for the humanist, another for the behaviorist, and other sets for the variations within each. Integrative frameworks are possible, however. One might be able to achieve fairly widespread agreement that disruptive behavior is typically a reaction to frustrated needs for esteem, self-worth, or autonomy. Teacher management techniques might then be viewed as activities which directly respond to these concerns; activities which tend to reduce patterns of inappropriate classroom behavior, increase academic and social skills and thus increase self-valuing and independent behaviors. And it is here that the discrete distinctiveness among the "schools of behavioral management thought" could be blurred. What teachers require is a flexible response-set, a repertoire of *alternative* courses of action, when faced with undesirable behaviors (Fink 1973). In this connection teachers must recognize the following principles:

1. Management techniques have no absolute vectors. A given management technique has no absolute effect upon a given pupil behavior. There are no absolute qualities such that we can predict an identical outcome for each utilization.

2. Management techniques are unlikely to be independent of each other. It is unlikely that any technique stands alone when evaluated for impact. The particular value of a technique may depend upon the context of other techniques within which it is used.

3. Consistency in management may not mean the repeated use of the same technique. Consistency refers to psychological and/or educational congruence and not the use of identical techniques.

The problems which arise from such a view are many, for trainers as well as teachers. This view suggests that objectives may differ from child to child within a class; for a given child from time to time; for different classes. Teachers must continually examine specific management objectives, matching problem with technique which requires appreciation of the range of values that can be attributed to any given intervention and the differential effects.

Therapeutic management techniques—those which (a) humanize the encounter between teacher and pupil behavior, (b) acknowledge differences in the meaning of deviance, (c) convey mutuality of respect, and (d) recognize needs of the social context—thus are vital elements of the teacher training curriculum. When management techniques are viewed from this perspective they become more than controlling activities. This is true for normal children; it is even more so for the disturbed. The more exposed "nerve endings" of the disturbed child require a teacher responsiveness molded to fit greater idiosyncrasy. Common problems, demanding common responses, exist, of course. The hallmark of the effective manager of behaviors, however, is the perceived need for interactions which accommodate greater variability in human behavior and are expressed by a fuller range of intervention options. These individuals recognize that meaning will be attributed to their intervention by the learners, and they should therefore be congruent with the total life of the classroom. Put another way, management techniques are not divorced or alien from the curriculum at large. What a teacher does in a management activity ought to be connected in a meaningful, natural way to the entire activity of the classroom. A management technique is an extension of the teacher as a person, and it behooves the concerned teacher to strive for personal consistency in teacher-pupil relationships, whether these are focused on the cognitive or the affective aspects of human experience. For many teachers, unfortunately, "management techniques" represent one domain and "learning" another.

The learning of the management experience may be viewed as an aspect of the total affective experience of the classroom. The regular classroom teacher who is asked for greater accountability in his or her dealings with the disturbed child will need to acknowledge *this* neglected aspect of human experience and to gain added skill in its application. Brown (1975) notes the many models which have developed under the rubric of the affective domain. No attempt to review these differences will be made here. The common thrust of all, however, is opposition to mechanistic models of pupil learning which exclude self-knowledge as a vital force in total learning. Derivations from affective theory that have particular utility for the teacher of the disturbed child in the regular classroom and which need emphasis are: (a) recognition of the potential for personal growth inherent in teacher-pupil relationships, and (b) the importance of a focus upon developmental concerns central to the lives of children.

It is important to stress that one set of assumptions which underlies affective education is that conflict-free children are those who think well of themselves, have satisfying relationships with others, and are in reasonable control of their own lives. Teachers who are to be effective in their efforts with the behaviorally disordered need to be trained in the skills and curricula appropriate to these objectives.

The themes of "behavior management" and, to a lesser extent, "affective education" have been stressed as the central learning issues for regular teachers in the mainstream. A shift in emphasis to these areas, which add crucial dimensions of experience and learning for the behaviorally disordered, in no sense invalidates the significance in teacher education of other substantive curriculum concerns subsumed under the

"Three R's." It is simply that a redress in balance is necessary—not a swing of the pendulum, but a shift in relative weight. The specialized nature of the issues which affect the behaviorally disordered who are to be mainstreamed requires this.

TEACHER PREPARATION—HOW?

A problem intimately connected to the content of training issue is that of the delivery system: how does one train teachers to be effective response agents to the behaviorally disordered? The answer is again in terms of the regular classroom teacher who, it is the argument here (given the assumption of the mainstreaming movement), occupies a more central place than previously in the process of educating disturbed children. While the focus will be upon regular education, its relevance for the training of all teachers who have roles with the emotionally disturbed will be obvious.

It is fashionable to criticize the nature of teacher education in America. The criticisms come from every corner—from those who participate as learners or instructors, as well as from those who provide financial support. Among the most trenchant and persistent criticisms of undergraduate teacher education are those dealing with the activities trainees undergo (Clark and Marker 1975). For the most part, future teachers learn to teach by being told about it rather than by the process of active participation. This theme—being lectured on and about teaching—is by far the most common means of teacher training across the country, while its illogic escapes few. The persistence of the pattern is remarkable.

With few exceptions, special education training patterns have followed the same model. The Bureau of Education for the Handicapped, concerned about this phenomenon, has placed considerable pressure upon training programs to increase practical training. This pressure has had some effect. Absolute time spent "in the field" is by itself no guarantee of training, however. The *integration* of theory and practice is required and is simply not well developed in undergraduate teacher education, regular or special.

The task faced by the regular classroom teacher in the mainstreaming of the disturbed is one of practice linked to theory. The management of disturbed children, whether viewed from the narrower perspective of behavioral control or the broader one of affective education, is an active task, for teachers must literally work with children who are "active behavers." The unfortunate experiences of so many teachers who try to teach difficult children is that their only basis for acting toward these children is theoretical. This is, again, a problem for the teacher. Unskilled, and therefore feeling incompetent and threatened, teachers engage in behaviors which they know best from the culture which has shaped them. Repressive and punitive acts follow. Rejection and exclusion become commonplace. The unhealthy cycle is repeated and reinforced by a school system which is unsure of itself in the face of disturbing behavior. So much for the education of the emotionally disturbed in the regular classroom!

The point is made. Regular teachers cannot be expected to do different things until and unless teacher educators do things differently. And what needs to be done differently?

It is not sufficient to provide regular classroom teachers with "input" about problem children, which has been a widely used strategy for bringing about the heralded interface between regular and special education. The theory-practice problem is not resolved by that process since "input" typically will represent "information about" rather than active learning. More significant are training approaches which make it possible for future teachers to acquire the "what" of special skills as an integrated part of their total training with systematic attention given to the ultimate functional demands to be placed upon the teacher in the classroom.

At Indiana University an innovative program for training undergraduate teachers of the mildly handicapped may be seen as an example of a solution to the problem of "active, integrative, knowing." This program, which has been evolving for several years, came about as a result of an internal reorganization of the teacher education function of the School of Education. This reorganization permitted the formation of *ad hoc* groups of faculty who could join together and assume responsibility for carrying through a training program for teachers. This group established a program which had as its formal training objective the training of teachers with certification both in regular and special education who would have skills to work in the classroom environment produced by mainstreaming. The program was built upon a model developed by M. I. Semmel and M. C. Sitko and reported in detail by Shuster (1973) which views teaching as "a performance skill learned best by practice and which provides accurate feedback about one's performance." Within this framework, learning about behavior management becomes a graduated set of experiences involving practice in simulated, controlled laboratory, and finally, natural classroom settings.

The advantages of simulated activities are many. Most important is the opportunity provided for risk-free trainee behavior, crucial to the development of behavior management skills (Fink 1973). Control over the learning environment is yet another clear advantage. This permits the simulation manager to guarantee the appearance of given children's behaviors, which one has no assurance will appear in the natural environment of student teaching. Future teachers can try out behaviors without loss of face or fear of reprisal—and most importantly—without *damage* to children.

There are many kinds of simulation formats that can be adopted. One method (Fink *et al.* 1974) stresses systematic role-playing of all participants in a semester-length "course" of behavior management training modules. Each module focuses upon some technique or strategy of behavior management and contrives situations for active participation. The variety of roles specified in each module—typically those of teacher, good pupil, deviant pupil, observer—enhances students': (a) awareness of different behaviors, (b) skill development in the use of management techniques, and (c) overall conception of classroom management.

The major purpose of the "role plays," however, is to place the student in a position to experience the many-sided aspects of the management problem. What does it feel like to be a student at the receiving end of "X" technique? What is the experience of the teacher using the technique? The importance of these experiences as the first major step in "active knowing" cannot be sufficiently emphasized. Students who enter the course will be far-removed from the realities of responsible behavior management. For the first time, perhaps, they will systematically confront their affective responses to the processes of deviancy and its active management. This experience will provide them with a real basis for learning. This awareness is linked to the development of specific management skills and their integration into a future response potential. This development is to a large extent idiosyncratic, however, since each trainee will experience and integrate those activities upon the basis of unique experience. The learning process is by no means purely experimental. Lectures and discussions, mainly the latter, complement but do not dominate the activity. These simulated activities then systematically emphasize: (a) sensitivity and awareness, (b) skill development, and (c) integration-evaluation of a wide range of behavior management contexts.

A second step in the development of "active knowing" about behavior management is developed through a controlled laboratory setting.

The Indiana program, through the Center for Innovation in Teaching the Handicapped (CITH), incorporates a Computer-Assisted-Teacher-Training-System (CATTS) in this laboratory which has as its most important function the provision to trainees of immediate feedback and analyses of behavior management activities. These behavior management activities are carried out in controlled settings—experimental classrooms or teaching stations which are incorporated within the laboratory. This feedback to trainees serves an important function; it provides objective, selected data which can be utilized by trainees and/or their supervisors in the modification of teaching behaviors.

This controlled laboratory setting provides additional advantages in the training of behavior management skills. In particular, trainees learn a wide variety of observation coding skills which adds unusual refinement to their powers of assessing needed interventions for students. Skill in observation is, in fact, a vital component of good behavioral management, a process which until recently has been largely ignored in teacher training curricula.

The progression of training through these activities thus provides a logical basis for movement into student teaching and the natural classroom. The students' sequential learning of behavior management techniques and their continued application as part of the total teaching process in the various laboratory settings may make even more significant than it is already, the "culminating" applied experience of undergraduate training.

TEACHER PREPARATION—WHERE?

The initial competency of classroom teachers is just that—a beginning set of skills which requires elaboration and refinement as everyday experience is encountered and accumulated. Within the context of mainstreaming this will mean greater demands from teachers for skills beyond those gained in even the most advanced preservice training programs. As teachers gain more experience in the classroom, new sets of training issus emerge, new questions arise. As new procedures and strategies are conceptualized for the behaviorally disordered, the on-line teachers develop greater needs for additional formalized learning.

Masters level programs offered at most colleges and universities are designed to fill such needs. Typically, a training format is offered which has remarkable similarity to its preservice cousin in being on campus and having lecture-discussion formats. The emphasis in training is likely to be abstracted from reality.

The radical response to the incremental training needs emphasized by mainstreaming is a deliberate and systematic movement of the training activity from the campus stage to the reality of the public school. In-service education which is typically carried out within the schools is *not* the model offered for emulation, however (Fink and Brown 1974). School-based in-service education typically suffers from numerous failings, a partial catalog of which follows: (1) insufficiency of resources, (2) inadequate expertise, (3) poor planning, (4) non-continuity, (5) inadequate time allotment, (6) omission of teacher planning, (7) failure to focus on actual teacher change, (8) inadequate rationales for instituting change, (9) poor logistics of time and place, (10) resource unavailability, (11) passive participation, and (12) lack of feedback.

Thus, as movement into the schools for training is deemed increasingly desirable, forms of *in situ* training must also be evaluated for their appropriateness and effectiveness. Teachers who are eager to improve their skills for working with the behaviorally disordered will find their learning optimized through on-site programs which systematically answer the weaknesses detailed above. The colleges and universities should not feel threatened by increased commitments to on-site training. On the contrary, higher education could well view this arena as a fruitful one and provide active leadership in program development. The relationships between campus and public school/clinical setting/residential centers will be strengthened, and natural, functional leadership should emerge. Campus activities may be supportive and generative; they cannot, however, carry the burden of training which is to have a major impact. Cogan (1975) notes the importance of identifying promising programs and suggests the need for systematic assessment, dissemination, and assimilation of effective programs. His analysis supports a commitment to the principle that in-service education is an unrealized potential in education which awaits innovation and systematic evaluation and diffusion paradigms.

In what way can in-service programs develop to insure that the problems identified above are not repeated? A number of recent developments in teacher education, special education, and instructional and computer technology offer a solution to many of the criticisms raised earlier by Fink and Brown (1974). The authors argue the value of taking advantage, first, of developments in performance-based programs focusing both on student and teacher behaviors which require change. Skill acquisition for teachers would be linked to desired change in student behavior. Teacher input into the definition of behavior to be changed or skills to be added is thus assured. Second, feedback on the effects of teacher interventions on pupil behavior could be built directly into training by application of The Computer-Assisted-Teacher-Training-System developed by Semmel (1968). This feedback may be instantaneous or delayed, and it deals with content that is teacher defined and planned. Actual participation of teachers is an integral part of the process. Finally, instructional development technology as applied to in-service education can make available to teachers a wide variety of instructional materials which may be selected for classroom use. This multiplies the options for effecting change in classroom practice, and since the options will be self-selected, individual teachers will be stimulated to define objectives and bring about change. Each of these emergent trends—performance-based programs, computer technology, and instructional development technology—provides important possibilities for meeting the educational needs of the behaviorally disordered. When combined and adapted for use in in-service education, they may serve to provide a powerful model for implementing training; a model which will overcome many of the standard, and justifiable, criticisms directed at field-based programs.

CONCLUSIONS

Providing educationally relevant solutions for the emotionally disturbed appears to be within reach, conceptually and technically. The fiscal variable must also be reckoned with, and it is here that the limitations of effectiveness in programming appear most obvious.

For the most part the "mainstreaming" movement is itself conceptually sound. It asks simply that children be maintained, insofar as possible, within regularized settings with a full panoply of support services. That does not seem to be a very new idea at all! Few of us would discourage that interpretation of mainstreaming. Less comfort would prevail, however, if mainstreaming implied automatic, uncritical movements of children without regard to the psychological and educational effects on the children concerned. Pressure upon the regular educational track to improve its potential for helping troubled youngsters is to be desired and implies a vigorous new look at our models for training both teachers and the individuals with whom they work in the service delivery system. The mainstreaming movement may have provided a much-needed and timely stimulus to look anew at the education of our teachers.

REFERENCES

Birch, J. W. *Mainstreaming: Educable Mentally Retarded Children in Regular Classes.* Reston, Va.: The Council for Exceptional Children, 1974.

Bower, E. M., and Hollister, W. G. *Behavioral Science Frontiers in Education.* New York: Wiley, 1967.

Brown, G. I. "The Training of Teachers for Affective Roles." In *Teacher Education: The Seventy-fourth Yearbook of the National Society for the Study of Education.* Part II. Chicago: University of Chicago, 1975.

Chaffin, J. D. "Will the Real Mainstreaming Program Please Stand Up! (or . . . Should Dunn Have Done It?)." *Focus on Exceptional Children* 6(5) (1974): 1–18.

Clark, D. L., and Marker, G. "The Institutionalization of Teacher Education." In *Teacher Education: The Seventy-fourth Yearbook of the National Society for the Study of Education.* Part II. Chicago: University of Chicago, 1975.

Cogan, M. L. "Current Issues in the Education of Teachers." In *Teacher Education: The Seventy-fourth Yearbook of the National Society for the Study of Education.* Part II. Chicago: University of Chicago, 1975.

Deno, E. N., ed. *Instructional Alternatives for Exceptional Children.* Arlington, Va.: Council for Exceptional Children, no date.

Dunn, L. M. "Special Education for the Mildly Retarded—Is Much of It Justifiable?" *Exceptional Children* 34 (1968): 5–22.

Fink, A. H. "Teacher-Pupil Interaction in Classes for the Emotionally Handicapped." *Exceptional Children* 38 (1972): 469–74.

———. *Behavior Management Training Program: Instructor's Manual.* Center for Innovation in Teaching the Handicapped, U.S. Office of Education, Bureau of Education for the Handicapped, Contract No. OEG 9-242178-4149-032, 1973.

———, and Brown, K. *A Model In-service Training Program for Training Teachers of the Behaviorally Disordered.* Center for Innovation in Teaching the Handicapped, U.S. Office of Education, Bureau of Education for the Handicapped, Contract No. OEG 9-242178-4149-032, 1974.

———, and Glass, R. M. "Contemporary Issues in the Education of the Behaviorally Disordered." In *The First Review of Special Education,* II, edited by L. Mann and D. Sabatino. Philadelphia Journal of Special Education Press, 1973.

————; Glass, R. M., and Guskin, S. L. "An Analysis of Teacher Education Programs in Behavior Disorders." *Exceptional Children* 42 (1975): 47–48.

Hewett, F. M., and Blake, P. R. "Teaching the Emotionally Disturbed." In *Second Handbook of Research on Teaching,* edited by R. M. W. Travers. Chicago: Rand McNally, 1973.

Joint Commission on Mental Health of Children. *Crisis in Child Mental Health: Challenge for the 1970's.* New York: Harper, 1970.

Long, N. J.; Morse, W. C.; and Newman, R. G. *Conflict in the Classroom: The Education of Children with Problems.* 2nd ed. Belmont, Calif.: Wadsworth, 1971.

Morse, W. C.; Cutler, R. L.; and Fink, A. H. *Public School Classes for the Emotionally Handicapped: A Research Analysis.* Washington, D.C.: Council for Exceptional Children, 1964.

Reynolds, M. C., and Davis, M. D. "Exceptional Children in Regular Classrooms." Minneapolis, Minn.: LTI/Special Education, 1971.

Semmel, M. I. *Project CATTS I: A Computer Assisted Teacher Training System.* In *Studies in Language and Language Behavior,* VII, edited by A. P. Van Teslaar. Center for Research on Language and Language Behavior. University of Michigan, 1968.

Shuster, S. K. "Special Education in Search of Change." *Viewpoints* 49(1) (1973) Bloomington: School of Education, Indiana University.

9

The Educational System

A. J. PAPPANIKOU
and
JEROME J. SPEARS

Throughout this volume one finds references to the negative effects of systems upon children and the concomitant need for system change. Pappanikou, Paul, and Rhodes specifically questioned the concept that one should mainstream children without first attending to the school environment with which the child *must* interact. If that milieu is not predisposed to change that would enhance the mainstreaming of exceptional youth, then efforts to reintegrate these children will fail.

The concepts of "reintegration" or "mainstreaming" imply that the system's policies and programs which were initially responsible for self-contained placement of a particular pupil needing special education are, at the time of reintegration, in concert with the child's individual needs. The school's personnel must be committed to individualized instruction and to the reintegration of that child into a regular classroom. The class must now project a more positive perception that that which was the case before the student's initial placement. If attitudes and programs do not manifest a readiness for reintegration, returning the child to the regular class renders little educational benefit to that pupil. It may, however, meet the system's needs to conform to the professionally accepted concept of mainstreaming as well as to meet the state's statistical requirements that are essential for reimbursement of funds. In addition, some systems have discovered that it can be less expensive to reintegrate the child than to provide special full-time services. For these systems, it also becomes profitable in that the state and federal reimbursements continue and/or increase.

This situation depends upon individual state regulations. For example, in Connecticut a school system presently receives 2/3 of *all costs* if a child is mainstreamed 1/3 or more of the school day. For self-contained pupils (children in a special education class more than 2/3 of each day) the system only receives a reimbursement of 2/3 of *excess costs*. However, there is at least one state whose policy is to cut off special education reimbursement once a child has been mainstreamed.

Thus, to legislate and, in turn, mandate the mainstreaming concept does not insure a successful reintegration of the concerned child. Too many systems have adopted the concept without adequate attention to program and curriculum revisions that are essential for system attitude change as well as a successful education experience for the child.

Integrating or reintegrating exceptional youth with "normality" are viable and essential processes. However, the manner in which these goals are achieved is in need of systematic planning.

Figure 9.1 presents a model for recycling a disturbed or disturbing child's behavior. The authors feel that this model explains what occurs in any attempt to modify behavior. It attempts to perceive the process from both the child's cognitive life space and that of the practitioner. The model is not allied with any specific approach for changing behavior. It only attempts to figurativecly depict the child's perception of those conditions that give rise to the formation and strengthening of disturbed and/or disturbing behavior. It further depicts the effects of intervention upon these conditions, again from the child's viewpoint.

The aim of any intervention procedure is to move a youngster away from the external cycle and toward the internal. This has always been the goal of any mental health effort, but modification of the behavior has traditionally been attempted via an analysis of the need structure and introspection thereof. The limited success of such strategies are well documented by Eysenck. In view of this, the last decade has been characterized by intervention techniques based upon learning theories. These techniques intervene somewhere in the outer or negative cycle so as to alter the child's behavior or habit in the direction of acceptability (inner cycle). It has been the intent of these interventions to help the child's human milieu reconstruct a positive image of him (1, 2, and 3 of Figure 9.1 depict this type of intervention and recycling procedure).

Thus, the new responses to the child should have the effect of positive reinforcement and should lead to a strengthening of the child's new behavior, albeit not the stronger of these two competing habits. Each

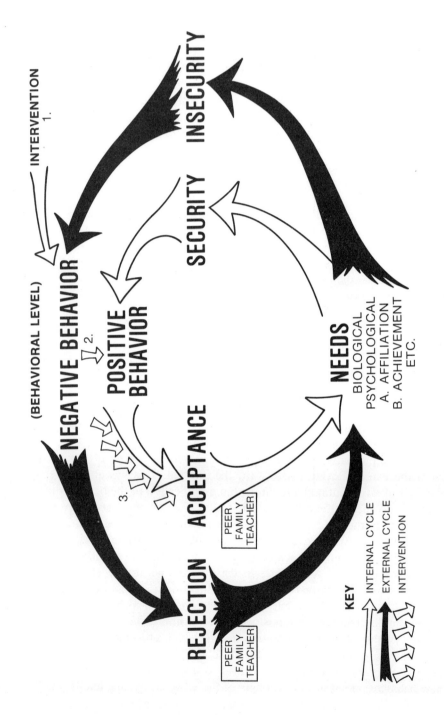

FIGURE 9.1. Behavior recycling for an individual disturbed/disturbing child.

time this occurs, however, the weaker, competing, acceptable, or correct habit will gain strength. Continuation of this cycle will increase the strength of the new habit. In time, under similar stimuli situations, it should become the more probable response. The principle of generalization then should allow for permeation to other situations.

In the initiating stage of recycling, these approaches may disregard the reasons for the behaviors. However, it is hypothesized that the cause or need underlying the cause will be resolved or met, respectively, if the new behavior (structured via intervention) leads to positive or pleasurable reactions from these individuals perceived by the child as most important (peer, family members, teacher).

One main objective of any attempt to modify an exceptional child's behavior is to reintegrate that child into normality or the mainstream. The attainment of this objective is not totally dependent upon the success of the intervention process upon the child *per se*. Of equal importance is the readiness of the system(s) with which the child must interact to change so that program modification, based upon the child's needs, may occur. Success of the reintegration process can occur only if both undergo change. For to change the child's behavior without changing the environment which was, in part, responsible for that behavior that excluded him is to negate the effects of the intervention efforts with the child.

It is therefore imperative that a systematic approach be developed to recycle or modify the system before or during the re-educational efforts with the child.

Since systems are represented by people, the process of recycling or changing the system is very similar to that depicted for a child in Figure 9.1. Changes in Figure 9.1's need structure, intervention agents, and human environmental reinforcers render a model for system change. This model is depicted in Figure 9.2.

Similar to the intervention process for individuals discussed earlier, the core of the model for system change is the physical need structure of the system or the psychological need structure of those individuals who represent the system. All of these needs, whether physical or psychological, mirror the need structure of the system representatives and, as such, are subject to a same process for change as was described earlier for a disturbed child.

However, unlike the model for individual behavior recycling, where intervention can be initiated anywhere in the cycle, the model for system change can most effectively be changed via intervention at the action level.

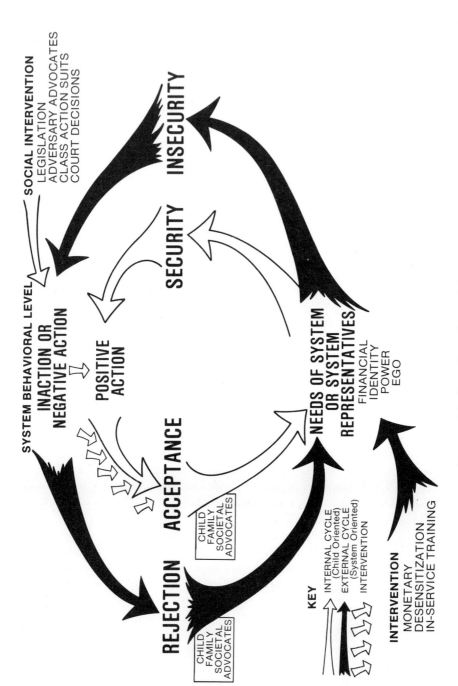

FIGURE 9.2. Recycling of a social system.

However, any intervention that takes place in the system recycling model has to concern itself with groups rather than with individuals. Even in cases where the system is autocratically administered, intervention with the autocrat alone does not insure complete system change unless the subordinates also undergo change. In the instance of a public school system, for example, commitment by a school board and superintendent to program change for the handicapped does not necessarily result in programmatic changes for these children. In order for this to occur, the various layers of administrators (supervisors and principals) as well as teachers must become committed so that the objectives of any policy change may be realized. Central office directives, aimed at mainstreaming exceptional children, do not by themselves bring about viable programming that results in perceiving the exceptional child as an extension of the normality continuum. In many cases these directives have the opposite effect, for, without a belief that the approach itself is viable, middle management and instructional personnel only go through the motions of mainstreaming which result in the physical mobility of the child into regular classes without addressing the concepts inherent in a successful mainstreaming venture. These include individualized instruction, curriculum change, and the marshaling of support services which help the teacher adjust to each child's strengths and weaknesses as well as his or her individual learning style.

Therefore, while intervention at the behavioral level engenders motivation for action at the central office level, there is no assurance that this action will programmatically affect the classroom. In order for this to occur, provisions must be made to meet the various needs of the system's middle management and instructional staff.

Based upon experiences with mainstreaming efforts in schools the authors believe that most motivation for change traditionally has been applied at the system behavioral level. This pressure has usually been engendered by adversary type intervenors which include the following:

1. Legislative action which mandates that the needs of exceptional youth are to be met in a continuum of services culminating in the re-integration of the child into normality. The most notable law in this regard is Massachusetts' Chapter 766 (1974). The due process requirements associated with this law mandates action by school officials toward the goal of reintegrating the child into the mainstream. The negative legal consequences associated with noncompliance render sufficient clout so that maximum motivation is engendered toward the goal.

2. In states where legislative action does not mandate mainstream-

ing, adversary child advocates may intervene to effect change in the system's programming efforts for exceptional youth. These advocates may be parents, friends, or associations which are allied with one or several categories of handicapped youth. Their approach is usually one that begins with parental requests for specific services or programs. This is usually at the level of the principal of the neighborhood school. Failure of the system to provide services at this level leads the parents to meet with the superintendent and board of education. At this level, the parents may request that representatives of a specific association accompany them to these meetings. Failure of the parents to request help does not rule out special interest group participation, for if the issue is one with which they identify, the group may independently enter the picture and support the parental requests.

3. If the board of education does not wish to embrace the changes implied in the parent and/or association request, then, that body may find itself as the defendent in a *class action suit*. The threat of litigation itself sometimes forces the system into positive action via *consent agreements*. These agreements may outline stipulations that must be met by a certain time, or litigation may continue. An excellent example of this is found in the class action suit between the *Rhode Island Society for Autistic Children, Inc., et al.* vs. *Board of Regents for Education for the State of Rhode Island* (1975).

4. If the litigation continues and there is a court decision in favor of the plaintiff, as was the case in *Pennsylvania Association of Retarded Citizens (PARC)* vs. *the State of Pennsylvania* (1973), then a master may be appointed by the courts to assure that the educational provisions of the court's decision are carried out.

In all of the above, the interventions are adversary in nature in that the initial impetus for change, that the system opposes, comes from outside of the system. As a result of adversary actions the system representatives who are forced to initiate a positive response are central office administrators. If they act only through administrative directives, there is little likelihood that the intent of the decisions will be translated into viable programs. It is only when the directives are buttressed with actions and programs aimed at meeting the needs of the individuals actually delivering services for the system, that the intended programmatic changes occur. Thus intervention at the system behavioral level without intervention at the Needs level lowers the probability of achieving the intended changes that have been articulated in court stipulations and, in turn, administrative directives.

It should be pointed out that there are occasions when intervention at the behavioral level results in programs which render highly valenced positive reinforcement (acceptance) from those most concerned by the changes in behavior of the system (child, family, social advocates). This positive reinforcement may lead to a satisfaction of the identity, ego, or other related needs that may be manifested in those representatives of the system who are responsible for direct pupil services. In these cases, it is possible to see system change (a movement from the outer cycle into the inner) without a concentrated programmatic effort aimed at meeting the *specific needs* of system representatives.

The authors' experience indicates that the probability of success with only adversary intervention plus reinforcement is not great. They have found that success, using this approach, is inversely related to the size of the system—the smaller the system the more successful will be the intervention at the behavioral level. But even in systems where some success has been attained, mainstreaming of the system into the inner cycle is definitely dependent upon the direct or indirect approaches which address themselves to meeting the needs of the system's representatives who are delivering services to exceptional youth.

Also, for success, interventions at the needs level must be supportive, trusting, and nonthreatening if they are to achieve their goal of maintaining or moving the system's representatives and the system into the inner or positive action cycle. It is only when such qualities are perceived in the intervention that those involved become secure and, thus, amenable to accepting change. Any threat at this level can only increase insecurity and lead to a strengthening of those perceptions which are not in the best interest of mainstreaming exceptional youth. The following interventions and rules for their application can be utilized at the needs level of Figure 9.2:

1. Additional services or money for supportive services and materials for regular teachers who are to be involved in the mainstreaming effort should be provided. These complementary entities should not be presented in a manner which may be perceived as bribes. They should be introduced as necessary additions to regular school programs that are involved in mainstreaming efforts.

2. Desensitization of negative perceptions of exceptional youth as sensitization toward a more humanistic and positive image must

be engendered. This should not be done so as to make the participants feel that the bulk of the problems to be resolved lie *within* themselves. The process should also be part of the total school program and should involve issues that are related to the total school population. Relating the process only to exceptional youth raises the probability of engendering insecurity and aggression and as such a continuation of negativism toward the goal of mainstreaming.

3. The in-service training component is one of the most important successful interventions. There are some very important steps that must be taken if the full impact of the training is to be realized. An in-service training curriculum that has been arranged by individuals other than the participants has less chance of successfully meeting the objectives than one where the individuals involved participated in the formulation of objectives. One of the better methods that the authors have utilized to ascertain the curriculum needs of the participants is to conduct a needs assessment. It should be stressed, however, that before any needs assessment is conducted, the participants manifest an inclination toward mainstreaming exceptional children. This perceived need may be created through the utilization of processes 1 and 2 noted above. In most cases all three approaches are essential in moving a system toward the positive cycle.

The following statements represent the most common issues that have been raised in needs assessment sessions with school personnel concerned with the initiation of mainstreaming:

1. Understanding of some of the behaviors of children, whether developmentally normal or abnormal.
2. Coordinating information about the child in terms of his own needs and those of the various subcultures with which the child interacts.
3. Making information in item 2 above meaningful to the teacher by having it presented in educational terminology.
4. How does one diagnose and prescribe?
5. Developing new approaches and materials to meet the individual needs of children. This should make use of 2 and 3 above.
6. How to organize and conduct case-study type meetings where teachers can learn more about the problems of children.
7. How to organize and conduct classes for elementary and junior and senior high school students in the area of human relations.
8. Effecting closer parent-teacher relationships via desensitization

of any hostilities that may be present in either or both; how to bring school and home together.

9. Helping the school staff, including the administration, in the development of sensitivity toward not only the child but the child's total milieu.

10. How to arrange for parent group meetings with discussion revolving around positive concepts relative to the handicapped.

11. How to change attitudes.

12. How to bridge the gap between the school and other community agencies working with atypical children.

To summarize, the models presented in Figures 9.1 and 9.2 attempt to relate people to systems. Attempts to implement a program based on the cycle presented in Figure 9.2 have been successful in rural and suburban school systems that were faced with the necessity of meeting the needs of exceptional children, within the context of "the least restrictive alternatives," in mainstream education.

MAINSTREAMING A SYSTEM

The following is a brief history of the process used to mainstream secondary schools in one district of a large urban school system. Each of the steps relates directly to the model presented in Figure 9.2, and each was initiated in a sequence determined by the perceived system needs and in response to pressures applied at the system behavior level.

The need for change in the direction of serving children in the mainstream of regular education, who had formerly been in self-contained and/or remote settings, was not an issue to the central office administration. The essential question was how to accomplish (1) staff attitude change at all levels, (2) program changes, (3) development of staff competencies to deal with new instructional problems, and (4) community support for those changes.

In terms of system needs, the following circumstances prevailed: (1) the system was operating within an existing budget which did not provide the needed funds; (2) the key moderator of change was the building's principal, for programmatic success within a school depended on his or her support; (3) a second important moderator of change was the union representing the teaching staff since any in-service training programs depended upon union approval; (4) constitutional guarantees of procedural due process required that parents become involved; and (5) lasting program change with movement toward a more normalized system for all children required the involvement of community leaders as well as children and school personnel who were not involved in special education endeavors.

The initial step in the change process was to provide fiscal resources to seed a uniquely Philadelphian mainstreaming effort. Therefore, twenty thousand dollars was awarded the system for this purpose from the University of Connecticut's Education Professions Development Act (EPDA) mainstreaming grant. This special award was provided on the condition that the monies be used to plan for and facilitate the mainstreaming of exceptional children and that the model for such be created by the Philadelphia school personnel. The project directors emphasized this point for it was essential that, at this stage and throughout the process, the critical decisions be made by system personnel rather than persons external to the system. It was believed that, for a program to succeed, the representatives of the system, at all levels, would have to have an investment in the project. Mainstreaming efforts where this was not the case produced less successful efforts. The second step was to provide key administrative personnel—including principals, directors of guidance, reading, and curriculum—with an explanation of EPDA's mission and objectives as they pertained to mainstreaming and Philadelphia. During this orientation the legal and philosophical orientations of mainstreaming special education children were presented. The aim of those discussions was to explain:

1. The need for the development of a mainstreaming model specific to the individual characteristics of the schools which would be involved relative to their community, school facilities, staff, and students.

2. The benefits which could accrue to regular teachers and students from changes in programs and attitudes.

3. The need for specialized technical assistance to counter strong resistance from instructional staff who opposed or were afraid of change.

Following the completion of this stage with administrators, similar orientation meetings and discussions ensued with the total staff and union representatives. Emphasis was placed on the principle that the only model that would succeed would be one developed by the staff of each school working together to satisfy each school's unique needs. Pursuant to this end a needs assessment via a modified Delbeque process was completed in each school. This procedure involved dividing school staffs into nominal groups of five or six who were asked to list the information or skills they considered essential to successful mainstreaming. These group lists were combined in a master list which was presented to the total staff. In this second phase each item was rank ordered in terms of its priority to the group. This master list then became the basis for planning the in-service program. In-service for staff at all levels was to be arranged by district personnel and paid for with the funds provided from outside the district (EPDA). The selection of speakers, the scheduling of meetings, and the reimbursement of participants according to union guidelines, was handled exclusively within the district. Workshops were held for administrators, special education personnel, and regular class teachers both jointly and separately, depending on the topics that the participants desired. In other words this was "their show."

Staff development sessions were open to parents and interested persons from the community. During these sessions it became obvious that many parents were reluctant to have their children moved from the protective atmosphere of the special education class into the regular class where they felt they would be exposed to the ridicule of other children and teachers. Involvement of these parents in sessions with school personnel was extremely beneficial because their dialog with teachers anticipated and prevented many adjustment problems when program changes actually occurred. Also, in terms of generating support for system change, the interaction of parents of non-special education children with teachers, consultants, and parents of exceptional children marked the first step in the "normalization" of the education system. It is strongly believed that one of the basic requirements for successful mainstreaming is that all individuals concerned with the school—parents, students, and educators—accept the principle that "normal" encompasses a great deal more than we have traditionally accepted.

The developmental steps outlined above were followed by the gradual implementation of the models developed for specific schools. Participation of teachers and students was on a voluntary basis. This voluntary participation insured that the individuals involved had a commitment to the success of the venture which would generate contagious enthusiasm. In addition, the success resulting from this commitment gave the model credibility with other staff members and led to requests for involvement from other staff. In a sense, the successful development and implementation of model mainstreaming programs became a status activity which appealed to teachers who initially tended to be somewhat skeptical of educational innovation.

Although this description of one attempt at system change is of necessity brief and fails to document adequately the efforts of many dedicated educators and parents, it does serve to illustrate how the recycling model presented in Figure 9.2 can facilitate change. The experience related here must be characterized as a success in terms of system change—a success which resulted from intervention both at the level of system behavior and system needs. If we are to effect "real" change rather than "apparent" change, as is so often the case, then attention must be given to resolving the identity, power, ego, and financial needs of those individuals who represent the system and who are the moderators of change.

MODEL FOR MAINSTREAMING

It seems only fitting that a discussion of individual and system change be followed with a model administrative structure which represents both a method for normalizing a system and a strategy for effecting individual change with the least stigmatization of children. It is the authors' belief that the continuity mainstreaming model illustrated in Figure 9.3 provides: (1) a maximum opportunity for the heterogenous interaction of children; (2) for the efficient ordering of services to provide for continuous progress from maximum to minimum intervention; (3) for minimal labeling and stigmatization of children; (4) a method for organizing different certificated specialists, such as learning disabilities teachers, social workers, and psychologists, to maximize effectiveness and minimize conflict. Point number four is particularly important to the cost efficiency and cost effectiveness of programs. One of the criticisms of the cascade of services model is that continuity is not stressed or even alluded to as a student passes from one service entity to the next. This apparent discontinuity often results in duplication of effort and ineffective communication between specialists.

The development of this model in the late 1960s was prompted by the realization that a complete and graduated range of services must be available if exceptional children are to be successfully moved into a normalized educational setting. Typically the movement of children into or out of the mainstream has been handled in a rather sudden and inflexible way. This is not to suggest that considerable thought is not given to these program changes, but rather that we have tended to think of interventions in terms of assignment to a "class" or a program instead of examining the possibility of gradually modifying the child's school experience along a continuum of options. Rather than planning for children in terms of a self-contained class, a resource room, or a regular class, this model provides a way to program for a continuous range of interventions and also a way to normalize a child's program as rapidly or as slowly as necessary without suddenly exposing the child to a totally novel situation.

In reading the following descriptions of the levels and the various roles associated with each, it is important to keep in mind that this is an ideal model and may therefore not be suitable, in unmodified form, for all districts. On the other hand, the authors would suggest that the concepts and procedures inherent in this model are applicable to any district. The successful use of the model is not dependent on providing four different types of classrooms with an adjacent diagnostic center, but, rather, success will depend on providing these coordinated services in some way so that a full range of options and resources are available when planning for exceptional children.

Briefly, Level I represents the regular class where support is provided in response to behavioral and/or academic deficits. This intervention is either direct or indirect, depending on the severity of the problem and the teacher's need for support. The progression of interventions ranges from a single teacher-consultant conference to the use of an itinerant teacher for a short period of time. Between these two extremes a total range of options exists. For example, a consultant can suggest a strategy for changing a child's behavior or for diagnosing an academic problem on the basis of what the teacher says; the consultant can observe the class in session and suggest changes in the teacher's behavior if this is a problem area; he or she can diagnose the child in class and suggest a different instructional approach or materials. The major point is that emphasis, at this level, is on providing the least conspicuous effective intervention; the objective is to maintain as normal a setting as possible. This Level I approach has a number of advantages. Services are available to all children on an as-needed basis. The identification of a child as different is minimized. Through contact and interaction with a consultant, regular class teachers are sensitized to the affective needs of children and are exposed to new methods and materials.

Level II represents a *diagnostic* and *resource* room where children can receive academic support on a short-term basis and where academic or behavior problems can be diagnosed. The role of the Level II teacher is to identify specific academic deficits and to indicate instructional methods or management techniques for use by a regular classroom teacher in Level I.

In the event a problem diagnosed by the Level II teacher cannot be

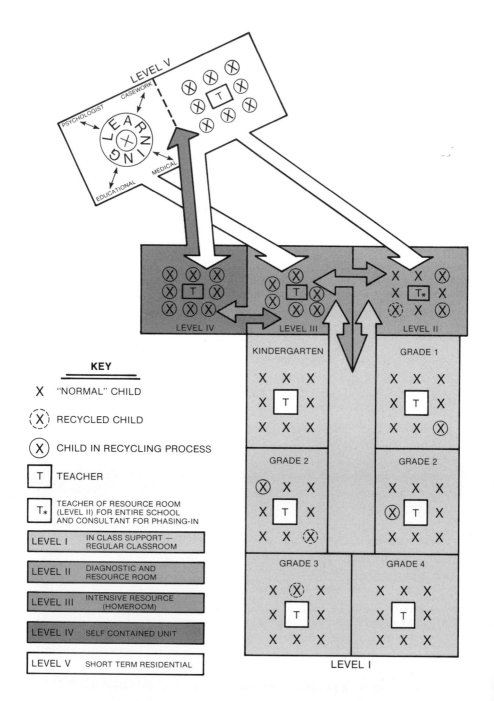

FIGURE 9.3. Continuity mainstreaming model.

dealt with in the regular classroom the Level III Resource Room would be utilized for part of the school day. The objective at this level is to move a child to mastery of an academic or behavioral task which presently interferes with learning in his or her regular class. Movement into the Level III resource room for a part of the school day is on a temporary basis. Movement from this level would either be back to Level I or to a Level IV resource room.

The function of the Level IV room is to manage behavior which is too severe for either a regular class or a Level III resource room. Level IV is not a terminal placement, and the management of behavior does not preclude academics. Rather, Level IV is a highly controlled self-contained setting where intensive academic instruction takes place in conjunction with the development of behaviors which will facilitate functioning in a regular class. The emphasis is on the development of group social skills through gradual infusion into a balanced group environment. Movement from Level IV would be gradually effected to the small, highly structured setting of Level III and from there, gradually, to Level I.

Level V provides an opportunity for a short-term residential placement for diagnostic purposes. A major feature of Level V is the availability of a controlled environment where extraneous environmental variables are removed and a child's functional level can be accurately determined. As the presence at this level of a psychologist, social case worker, educator, and physician, suggests, the strategy is to involve an interdisciplinary team in the planning of educational programs based upon the learning style of the child. A classroom is available for the diagnosis of the child's ability to function in different academic settings. In this highly controlled environment it is often possible to identify teacher behavior or classroom characteristics which are antagonistic to a child and which can be avoided when the child later moves into a regular class. Here manipulation of both the child's characteristics and the environment takes place to ascertain the most appropriate educational strategy. After this has been accomplished the child is returned to the school from which he was sent with a liaison teacher whose function is to demonstrate the successful strategies and curricula that were developed as a result of the dual manipulation mentioned to above and to serve as the child's advocate.

It should also be pointed out that Level V can serve effectively as a halfway house to facilitate the movement of children from an institution into public schools. Too often this type of reintegration is attempted without adequate planning and without providing the child with an opportunity to adjust to the new surroundings. By using the Level V unit as a residential facility the child's movement into a regular school setting can be gradual and well planned.

Although the preceding discussion is brief, the reader will realize that, within this model, a total progression of interventions is available. At the same time the emphasis is on making the system responsive to the needs of different children rather than forcing children to fit the system. The focus is always on success, with a wide range of behaviors being dealt with in the regular class as part of the normal continuum of behaviors exhibited by school-age children. This has the dual benefit of providing additional resources to teachers to help them adjust instruction and curriculum to improve learning for children presently called "normal" while also serving children currently labeled as "exceptional," in a regular education setting. For those children whose behavior is sufficiently aberrant to warrant a label of "exceptional," a change in behavior will be effected but the change will be less of a forced change and more the child's positive response to an environment which perceives him (and is in turn perceived by him) in a positive way.

In actual use this model has demonstrated a considerable amount of flexibility. In rural settings the functions of Levels I, II, and III have been provided by a well-trained teacher within a single room with Levels IV and V available on a regional basis rather than within a district. In larger urban and suburban settings all levels except V have been provided within single schools. In these instances Level V is available, without residential facilities, for all schools in a single district. This approach has also been used with success on the secondary level, where large size has been an advantage in terms of course and scheduling options and in providing a choice of teacher personalities and instructional methods.

Before concluding the discussion of this model some comments relative to self-containment are in order. Certainly it is safe to say that the self-contained unit, which is an integral part of this model, is not currently in vogue. Special education, in its efforts to adequately meet the requirements of the law relative to providing exceptional children with the "least restrictive" alternative, has tended to deny the efficacy of a self-contained placement for children. For behavior-disordered children the discarding of this particular resource is likely to have disastrous consequences. It is necessary at times, notwithstanding the desirability of exposure to normal models, to control behavior through the use of a highly structured, stable environment. If one attempts to use self-containment as a permanent or terminal placement for children, then criticism is justified, but if this placement is temporary, for the purpose of providing the child with a positive social and/or academic experience, then criticism is inappropriate. The reality of dealing with children who, often over a long period of time, have developed severe maladaptive behavior is that the prevailing negative cycle must be broken. Some context to provide an initial positive experience, in an academic setting, must exist if we are to begin to change the child's perceptions of himself and society's perceptions of him. The administrative model presented here is conceptually grounded in the behavior recycling paradigm presented in Figure 9.1, where the basis for success is the elicitation and reinforcement, through acceptance, of an initial positive behavior (see Pappanikou *et al.* 1974).

SUMMARY

In the process of mainstreaming exceptional children the focus of attention must extend beyond the individual child. Most children no longer in mainstream education, or who are tagged for future removal, are children for whom the system does not work. To plan for the maintenance of these children in a regular class, without attempting to change the educational environment which has already failed then, is totally illogical. The models for individual change and system change presented in this chapter suggest procedures for effecting the necessary mutual accommodation of systems and individuals.

When discussing system change it becomes apparent that those persons who comprise the system have needs which, as they are met or not met, tend to influence system behavior just as an individual's needs effect his or her behavior. In the instance of individuals, change is most successfully effected by intervention at the behavior level while for systems this does not seem to be the case. For a system where there is usually considerable distance between decision-makers and the individuals who deliver direct services, input is needed at both the behavior level (decision-makers) and the needs level (non-decision-makers comprising the system). If this approach is not utilized, then the change which seems to occur is typically change for appearance and does not involve any real attitude or behavior change on the part of most members of the system.

The system change model presented in this chapter has the advantage of involving all individuals in the decision-making process, which results in each individual developing an investment in success. It is the author's contention, based on experience in a variety of educational settings, that this approach must be utilized to create a more normalized educational environment if exceptional children are to be returned to a mainstream where they have a chance of survival.

REFERENCES

Deno, Evelyn. "Special Education as Developmental Capital." *Exceptional Children* (November 1970): 229–37.

Eysenck, H. J. "The Effects of Psychotherapy." In *Handbook of Abnormal Psychology,* edited by H. J. Eysenck. New York: Basic Books, 1961.

Massachusetts Comprehensive Special Education Act of 1972 (Chapter 766).

Pappanikou, A. J., *et al.* Approaches Leading to Prevention of Emotional Disturbance in Children in Rural School Settings. Unpublished investigation, University of Connecticut, 1968.

Pappanikou, A. J.; Kochaneck, Thomas T.; and Reich, Melvyn L. "Continuity and Unity in Special Education." *Phi Delta Kappan* 55 (8) (April 1974): 546–48.

Pennsylvania Association for Retarded Children v. *Commonwealth of Pennsylvania,* 334F. Supp. 1257 (E.D. Pa. 1971).

Rhode Island Society for Autistic Children Inc., *et al.* v. Board of Regents for Education for the State of Rhode Island, C.A. 5081. (Stipulation between plaintiffs and defendant, Donald Taylor, 7-19-75).

Index

137

MAINSTREAMING EMOTIONALLY DISTURBED CHILDREN

was composed in 10-point Linotype Times Roman, leaded two points,
with display type in handset Times Roman by Joe Mann Associates, Inc.;
printed offset on Hammermill 55-lb. Lockhaven by Wickersham Printing Co., Inc.;
Smyth-sewn and bound over boards in Columbia Bayside Linen
by Vail-Ballou Press, Inc.;
and published by

SYRACUSE UNIVERSITY PRESS

SYRACUSE, NEW YORK